UNWAVERING
FAITH

JEANNIE BURGOS

BALBOA.PRESS
A DIVISION OF HAY HOUSE

Balboa Press books may be ordered through booksellers or by contacting:

Balboa Press
A Division of Hay House
1663 Liberty Drive
Bloomington, IN 47403
www.balboapress.com
844-682-1282

Scripture quotations marked NIV are taken from the Holy Bible, New International Version®. NIV®. Copyright © 1973, 1978, 1984 by International Bible Society. Used by permission of Zondervan. All rights reserved. [Biblica]

Scripture quotations marked NLT are taken from the Holy Bible, New Living Translation, copyright © 1996, 2004, 2007. Used by permission of Tyndale House Publishers, Inc. Carol Stream, Illinois 60188. All rights reserved. Website

Unless otherwise indicated, all scripture quotations are from The Holy Bible, English Standard Version® (ESV®). Copyright ©2001 by Crossway Bibles, a division of Good News Publishers. Used by permission. All rights reserved.

Scripture quotations marked NKJV are taken from the New King James Version. Copyright © 1982 by Thomas Nelson, Inc. Used by permission. All rights reserved.

Print information available on the last page.

ISBN: 978-1-9822-6461-1 (sc)
ISBN: 978-1-9822-6463-5 (hc)
ISBN: 978-1-9822-6462-8 (e)

Library of Congress Control Number: 2021903678

Balboa Press rev. date: 12/28/2021

To my daughters.

They have encouraged and inspired me to persevere in creating this inspirational gift. They believed in me through loss, divorce, heartbreak, and countless challenges. Their boundless patience helped me achieve my aspiration of becoming a published author. And their support has been paramount and forever embedded in my heart. Thank you, Kristen and Briana. You have taught me the true meaning of unwavering faith. May you journal life into your day and follow your passion. May you orchestrate your steps, revel in the moment, live in gratitude and love wholeheartedly. May you learn and grow from mistakes, forgive quickly and create a life of blissful memories. I love you immensely.

CONTENTS

ACKNOWLEDGMENTS

This book would not have been possible without the help of many people and dear loved ones. I would first like to acknowledge and humbly thank God for guiding me and holding me through this endeavor. He is unconditional truth and the provider of *all* understanding, and He has gifted me with a tenacious spirit to continue to strive no matter the adversity. Through unwavering faith, I have developed the inner strength to pursue my dreams. I am forever grateful.

I would like to lovingly acknowledge my grandmother Maria Teresa; my mother, Rosa Maria; and my departed father, Juan Antonio, for their love, praise, insight, and influence. I am grateful to them for always keeping me in their sacred prayers. Their belief gave me the energy to strive for more and keep the faith alive. I love you more than words could ever express.

Heartfelt thanks to my sisters, Glendaliz and Omayra; my nephews, Robert and Brandon; my nieces, Rosemary, Zelina, Ziara, Gianna and Ava; and my beautiful family for their love, support, soft place to fall and devoted bond. I am grateful and blessed to call you family.

I would like to thank my sister-friends Lisa, Awilda, Aleida, and Haydee for being there for me through childhood, marriage, children, divorce, singlehood, and wise-hood. Thank you for the encouragement and reinforcement. Priceless.

I am respectfully grateful to the inspirational guide masters of the world for guiding for good, better and best. Their open hearts and instrumental insight have ignited the fire within me throughout the years. I am so thankful to the teachers and up-lifters who reminds us that we are unstoppable and capable to reach our dreams in vivid color.

My sincere appreciation to all who were not named—my nearest and dearest, incomparable bosses, devoted friends, caring associates, and treasured loved ones. Thank you.

INTRODUCTION

Unwavering faith is an unshakable, steadfast, solid belief that you can achieve all that you desire. It is the confidence that you can make your dreams come true through devotion, dedication, and focus. It allows you to hone your thoughts, channel your emotions, and direct your heart toward your purpose.

Having unwavering faith expands your vision for a bigger, brighter, and better today. It gives you the inner passion and drive to reach the desired destination of your ideal tomorrow. The intent of this guided journal is to help you set out on your envisioned path.

Begin your journey and open your eyes to life's beauty. Be thankful that God's love can be found even through challenges and obstacles, through conflicts and struggles, and through loss and sorrow. Do not allow pessimistic inner chatter to cloud your mind with worry and doubt, for it merely invites the universe to manifest negativity in your life. Problems are there to be solved. They are there to teach you and help you grow. Keep your eyes uplifted and move forward along your path.

Unwavering faith opens your heart and mind to your unique spirit. It keeps you focused on your passion. It guides your steps closer to your goals and desires. The reality is this: You write the story, whether you are aware of it or not. Allow your inner spirit to lead you to your greatness. Don't give your pen to someone who will script your days away. Attaining unwavering faith opens your heart to the signs that the universe is sending you.

Unwavering faith guides you to your higher self. It directs you to be selfless, gracious, and grateful for both the positive and the unfavorable events in your life. God offers new lessons every day so that you may learn to overcome and reach a new tomorrow.

The blessings of unwavering faith unfold in sweet abandon as you become aware of the kindred spirits that are all around you. Happiness will follow you; open yourself to the sources of love that are present in your life. Trust in the extraordinary favor that surround you day in day out.

To have unwavering faith is to believe in the unseen. Believe deep in your core that what you wish—what you desire—will come to fruition. Your targets will manifest in due time. When your intent is absolute and your belief is heartfelt, you will come into what you ask for in conclusive form.

This I wish for you. May *Unwavering Faith* open your heart to the promising new tomorrow that lies ahead of you. You are the designer of your life—write your masterplan and follow it through. May you love with full abandon, and may God guide you along your path.

HOW TO USE THIS BOOK

This book was written to be a monthly guided journal of contemplative practice. You may read it cover to cover for the wisdom contained within; you may read it each month and follow the exercises step-by-step; you may read it with friends in a book club or study group and support each other through the process. You may use it any way that you desire. It is up to you. No matter how you choose to utilize this book, you will find within it the freedom to design your life.

This book is divided into twelve chapters by the months of the year, focusing on unwavering faith in areas such as prosperity, inner freedom, unconditional love, forgiveness, gratitude, courage, full abundance, passion, joy, wisdom, empathy and compassion, and the spirit of generosity.

Each chapter offers exercise prompts, a space for journaling, inspirational quotes, music playlists, original poetry, and real-life stories of unwavering faith. There are daily, weekly, and monthly assignments—some more intense than others—which allow you to explore that month's topic of personal development. Some of these exercises may provide the exact remedy to a situation that you have needed to resolve or heal in your life.

I wrote this book based on my own experiences with unwavering faith. To inspire, to bring peace, joy, love, awareness, and growth and, most of all, forgiveness. This book is not intended as a foretelling device—it is a work-in-progress gift for yourself. It is a device that will help you move in the direction of your intended desire. The goal is to help bring clarity to issues from your past so that you may address them from a place of peace. Challenge yourself and go through this guided journal with another (spouse, partner, sibling, friend, confidant), it may help you relate on a deeper level and connect through your shared experiences. However you decide to use *Unwavering Faith*—in meditation, in prayer, in intentional forgiveness—may you embrace it, enjoy it, and discover the exceptional you. Many blessings.

Photo by Jeannie Burgos

CHAPTER 1

January: Prosperity

But when you ask, you must believe and not
doubt, because the one who doubts is like a wave
of the sea, blown and tossed by the wind.
—James 1:6, NIV

For the Month of January

Open yourself to the blessings of prosperity. Ask to have plenty—so you may bless others and open the windows of abundance in all areas of your life. This will offer the freedom to fulfill dreams and the joy that evolves from giving. Prayer, meditation, and contemplation will keep you faithful to your beliefs. Open yourself to receiving God's gifts, and trust that He will deliver to you in ways that are greater than you can imagine. Recognize that God's miracles are all around you. The universe is waiting to pour its abundance out to you. When you knock, the doors will open. Breathe deeply in faith, and allow the answers to come forth. You have the ability to make it happen, and God will be there to hold you through it all. Be ready to receive the new wealth that will come to you. God will bless you in magnitude to your belief, so keep your faith in the forefront of all you do.

People often say to me, "I have prayed for prosperity, but I haven't received anything yet."

My response is, "What are you thinking of most? Are you focusing on the fact that you don't yet have what you want? Or are you trusting and having faith that what you pray for will come to you?" It is important to be patient and faithful. Don't stress or feel rushed, for that will only deepen your anxiety and waste your energy.

Believe that you will have more than enough, and open your heart to generosity. Call a friend, and treat your friend to something fun. Give to a local charity. Offer to help a stranger in need. Pray for others with gratitude in your heart. The prosperity that you give, you will get back in great quantity.

To Achieve Prosperity through Unwavering Faith

Allow yourself to receive without excuses or apologies. To live a life worth living, fully engaged, and making the world a better place for all those around you. You may have been conditioned to think that, no matter how hard you work, prosperity is extremely difficult to obtain. Clear your mind of old beliefs and focus only on good and deserving success. Wherever your thoughts go, that is what you become.

Pray earnestly for what you want, and wealth and riches will show up in many forms. Much of your success will come from the positive change in your attitude and your state. Trust in your intuition, and follow the direction of your heart. Commit to what brings you happiness, and focus on the sweet pleasure of wanting what is good for yourself and others. When your deeds bring joy to you and those around you, this alignment will bring happiness and abundance into your life. Trust that prosperity is in your future. It is your destiny. If you don't see it right now, have faith that it is on its way.

Thought

Think about what success means for you, and be intentional with your desire. Some examples of success are owning your own home, living debt-free, running your own business, achieving upward advancement at work, completing a new degree, having a successful relationship, being a good parent, or anything else you want to achieve. Understand how you want success to manifest for you, and envision yourself successful.

Words are tangible things, and the more you say them, the more they develop into your core beliefs. Pray, contemplate, script, and meditate on the words that you want to turn into reality. Believe in your desires with your whole heart, and God will carry you to your goal.

Ask yourself, *What steps must I take to make my dream come true?* Write out those steps in the form of UPLIFT goals—which can be described as unique (distinctive), possible (promising), leverageable (influential), intentional (deliberate), faith-filled (confident), triumphant (victorious). If you want to achieve a dream within a year, break that down into a month-to-month plan. Ask yourself, *What do I need to accomplish each month to achieve what I want in twelve months?* Then break that down further, and ask yourself, *What do I need to accomplish each week?* When you organize your goals into reasonable and achievable pieces, suddenly a dream that seemed like a distant star becomes something that is within your grasp.

If you don't achieve your dream within your timeline, don't let that discourage you, but encourage you that you may need to make a progression correction. With each set back or disappointment, we have the opportunity to learn new life lessons. Ask God to be your guide and to show you which direction to go. Listen for His whisper, and open your heart to your intuitive wisdom.

Meditate on what you want to accomplish, and you will begin to see the opportunities that God places in front of you every day. When you change your belief from scarcity to prosperity, you open yourself to receiving God's blessings.

Truth in Wisdom

What I have experienced to be true is that the most important time of my life is right now. It's not in the someday; it's here in the present moment. If prosperity is what you desire, don't you want it now? What are you waiting for?

Remember, if you don't direct your steps, other people will. You will then wind up wandering off course and living according to someone else's goals and desires. Planning your life's direction is like charting a course on a map. Follow the route that you have drawn, allowing for inevitable detours, and keep going until you get to your destination. When you don't plan your path, you may end up drifting and lost.

I have learned to stop excusing my life away and settling for just barely scraping by. I open myself to prosperity so that I can help the people who matter to me and donate to causes that make a difference. Make a change using the abilities you have been given. We all have that power within. Believe that you can accomplish what you have set out to do, even when it is difficult. Decide that you want things that are different and better. You can't come back to life and do it all over again. The time is now.

Trust in Action

Everybody says to live in the present, but how do we do that? Each morning this month, take fifteen minutes after you wake up. Look inward and say to yourself, *Today is the best day of my life.* Let that sink in. Then say to yourself, *Wow, this is going to be the best day of my life! So, what am I going to commit to in order to make that happen?*

What do you want your today to look like? Are you going to have unexpected wealth coming in today? Are you going to meet incredible people today? Are you going to learn something life changing today? Are you going to have an amazing day at work today? Make this day beautiful, delicious, and bright. When you start believing in the possibilities of today, opportunities will manifest for you, because you will have committed to finding prosperity in the present moment.

All the shoulds, coulds, and what-ifs of life distract us and stop our forward motion. Life happens in the present tense. We take one step and then another step, live one moment and then another moment. When you shift your focus to moments that are joyful, you will live in a beautiful state filled with wonder and gratitude.

On the weekends, take an extra thirty to sixty minutes and meditate with tunnel vision on where you want your life to be. Feel it as if it has already come true. Be excited about it. Feel in your heart that this is the best time of your life, because you are going to make it so. Even if all the things you have prayed for don't show up today, the fact that you are in a joyful state allows you to ask for them the next day and the next.

As with all things in life, prosperous thinking takes practice. You can't learn the piano in one lesson, and you can't become fit in one workout. Each day, focus your mind on what you desire. Celebrate abundance as if it is already here. And know that, one day, it will be. Pray to receive prosperity for the good of others, and good is sure to come to you.

Visual Belief

In your mind's eye, picture a time when you needed to navigate to a destination. Maybe you were driving your car. Or if you don't usually drive, maybe you were navigating for the person behind the wheel. Either way, you were responsible for choosing the route that you would travel. Before you started driving, you made a plan for how you were going to reach this destination.

This is your mission for the month of prosperity. Maybe your desire is to be debt-free. Maybe you want to have enough resources to help your parents in their retirement. Maybe you want to buy a new house or pay off the mortgage on your existing home. Whatever your destination is, you are going to map out the road to get there.

When you are deciding on your route, focus on future planning to avoid future worrying. Maybe your worries are that you'll never experience financial freedom, that you'll never get married, or that you'll never accomplish your career goal. When you focus on your fears, you increase the likelihood of them coming true. They become self-fulfilling prophecies. Instead, use your resources to chart a reasonable and achievable pathway to reach your ambition. When you spend your energy planning instead of worrying, you'll manifest the outcomes that you want.

Once you head out on the road, you'll usually encounter some obstacles along your way. There will be traffic that slows you down, you will come across detours that change your course, or a quick stop for a beverage or bite to eat. No matter what may come or the time you arrive, you are committed to this journey, and you know that you will get there.

The route to prosperity is no different. Choose a destination. Plan your course. And know that, somewhere along the way, there will be detours. Learn from those who have blazed a prosperous path. Study from the best and learn their strategies. Reach out to successful people in your field and interview them to learn what has worked for them. Read biographies and attend seminars. You can educate yourself quickly, and before you know it, you're on your way to your destination.

When you are traveling on your path to prosperity, there will be times when all you want to do is stop and rest. If you want to make $250,000, tell yourself that you're going to donate a percentage of that money to charity. Imagine the joy and fulfillment you'll feel when you get to donate $25,000 to children with cancer or whichever charity speaks to your heart.

Recognize

If you find yourself in any degree of poverty, understand that poverty is a belief system that alters the way you see the world. In order to change your circumstances, you must first change your mindset. Fill your cup with the belief that prosperity can come into your life through unwavering faith. Prosperity is all around you. You see it every day. It's close enough to grasp. It's not a distant star; it's here now.

Prosperity manifests itself by way of your talents, abilities, and creative ideas that are longing to express themselves. Ask God to show you your talents. Ask Him to give you opportunities to utilize your abilities. There are gifts He gave you that will allow you to be a blessing to others. As you manifest these gifts, you will start believing in yourself more.

Even if you know what your abilities are, you may be afraid to bring them forth. We are often plagued by insecurities, and we can be our worst critic. Recognize the lies that you use to diminish yourself, and instead look at yourself in all your creative glory. You have talents that will help you walk a path of abundance. Embrace the creative soul that you are. Your attitude, your thoughts, and your unwavering faith are your connecting links to prosperity.

True Story of Unwavering Faith

Many of us have experienced moments of favor and overflow, with seasons of prosperity and good fortune. We have also been worn down by years of scarcity and lack. My journey in 2009 was a massive whirlwind of it all.

I was going through a divorce and began raising my two daughters on my own. I managed two investment properties that were in the process of foreclosure, and I was laid off unexpectedly. In the midst of this chaos, I suffered a health scare that brought me to my knees. I was drowning in the icy cold waters of hopelessness. My faith was all I had to hold onto.

I released my burdens to God, and I prayed with every ounce of conviction that I could muster. *I prayed my way out.* I applied what I learned through my spiritual journey—I opened my heart and continued forward with blind trust. I relied on my faith to guide me through this storm of fear and despair. I was focused on my longing for a better life, and I knew that this journey would be transformational. With unwavering faith, I knew I would conquer my worries and manifest my desires.

This did not come overnight. The lessons I learned opened up a side of me that I didn't know existed. I found the raw, true me—the woman I always wanted to be but was hesitant to become.

Every day, I launched my heart in gratitude for what I already had. Gratefulness slowly removed the negative outlook and neutralized the sadness. I didn't fully understand the importance and power of gratitude at the time; I simply knew it was something I had to do for my soul. Blind faith gave me the vision to see that God would bring me through. As I began surrendering it all to Him, doors started opening for me. Opportunities and interviews lined up, and the properties I managed received offers and were sold before foreclosure proceedings took place. I took time every day to give thanks for the new chapter in my life. With tears of appreciation to God, I realized that I had to let go of the old to make room for the new.

> *Do not be anxious about anything, but in every situation, by prayer*
> *and petition, with thanksgiving, present your requests to God.*
> —Philippians 4:6, NIV

Songs for Prosperity

Begin your journey to prosperity with gratitude and affirmation. Here is a powerful song of faith, along with an instrumental selection and two secular hits to help you focus as you journal:

- o *Song of faith*
  - – "The Story's Not Over" by Jeremy Camp
- o *Instrumental music*
  - – "Fearless Motivation" by Walter Bergmann
- o *Secular songs*
  - – "Champion" by Carrie Underwood, featuring Ludacris
  - – "Feel This Moment" by Pitbull, featuring Christina Aguilera

Journaling for Prosperity

I believe and receive prosperity with unwavering faith and envision my life today as:

_____

_____

_____

_____

_____

_____

Do your best not to worry about the future. Instead, focus on what you desire in immediate expectancy. You will see miracles manifest, seemingly out of thin air. As you receive God's blessings, give sincere and heartfelt thanks, and extend this desire for prosperity unto other people in your life. Wish them love, joy, peace, health, and wisdom, and you will see these blessings flow back every day of your life.

Manifestation begins with unwavering faith.
—Jeannie Burgos

Poem for Prosperity

Why do we believe prosperity to be a distant star?
A light that shines for others and ignores where we are.
Yet it is available for *all* to receive.
We can attain the riches we choose to believe.

What if we hold firm to the truth of our birthright?
What if we believe in God's affirmation and promise with *all* our might?
That we may *all* prosper, grow, and lead others with our light.

Why not change the old belief from defeat to possibility?
Why not live in peace, clarity, and realize new opportunities?

For prosperity is meant for *all* to achieve
We must believe to succeed, and it will manifest in maximum velocity.

Photo by Jeannie Burgos

CHAPTER 2

February: Inner Freedom

For we live by faith, not sight.
—2 Corinthians 5:7, NIV

For the Month of February

Trust that it is necessary to shed your old skin to achieve your ultimate growth. Be in the present moment and notice that you are still breathing, you are alive, and you are loved. Understand that, in order to flourish, you may lose some of the relationships that no longer fit the new you. The process of rebirth takes time. It has taken you years to create the person you have become, so shedding that old skin does not happen overnight.

Your old beliefs will keep you trapped until the day you open your eyes and realize that you are not living the life that you desire. It takes strength and authenticity to acknowledge your state of happiness, who you are within, and aspire to become.

What do you need to do in order to come into yourself? Allow yourself to see the person you are in all your complexity—the good, the broken, the wise, and even the misguided. Welcome the lightness that comes when you embrace vulnerability and release the many layers of defenses that have covered you. Take time to learn more about yourself so that you know what aspects of your authentic self you want to embody. Open yourself to new possibilities in life.

Release the negativity of your past and follow your own brilliance. Take one step followed by another step, and you will steadily get to where you want to be. You may have a secret wish that you want to fulfill. Don't hesitate—go for it! Don't allow your past to keep you prisoner from what can be yours. If your current path does not excite you or lead toward a goal that you desire, open your eyes to possibilities and seek a different path. If your future isn't directed by you, then who will direct it?

To Achieve Inner Freedom through Unwavering Faith

Skyrocket up the staircase to reach the new you. Let go of disappointments, which obstruct your growth and keep you from shedding your old self. It's easy to look up the stairway of life and feel daunted by the number of steps that stretch up into the distance. You might feel worried that you're supposed to get to the top. Calm your fears. You will not reach the top, for there is no end point during our lives. You will discover many landings on this journey that mark milestones and celebrations in your life. Your path to achieving inner freedom is in the climb itself.

When you shed the old, you will find yourself in a place that is unfamiliar and exciting. Let the excitement guide you. You might not notice the changes in yourself at first. Others will likely notice the differences before you do. People you know may tell you that they notice a different spring in your step or a new sparkle in your eyes.

It is helpful to journal during this phase. This is a way to record the changes you are experiencing in real time. You will be able to look back later and see the transformation that you've gone through. As you shed the layers of yesterday, remember that mistakes are made to teach you; they're not meant to keep you trapped as a prisoner of your old shortcomings. Perhaps you're holding onto something that happened years ago, and you don't recognize how much you've grown since then. You may find yourself keeping certain mistakes in the forefront of your mind, and thinking about them over and over. Forgive yourself for your mishaps and give yourself permission to learn from them so you can move forward.

Meditate, pray, and contemplate so you can go within and let go of whatever is holding you back. Take quiet moments for yourself. A place of solitude allows you to see yourself without the usual distractions and interruptions. Be steady and intentional, and soon you will be walking into the extraordinary life you have always desired.

Thought

Allow room for error and be gentle with yourself. Mistakes and stumbling blocks teach you what you must learn to get to the next level. At times, we play events over and over in our mind. We obsess over all the things that we should or shouldn't have said or done. All the "shoulds" and "coulds" cloud our thoughts and distract us from our purpose.

Each time we choose not to forgive ourselves, we add a brick to the weight that we carry within us. We add one brick and then another, and soon we are unable to move. We feel burdened by the weight of our mistakes. Learn your lessons, dust yourself off, and get back up again. Keeping yourself trapped in the past helps no one, least of all yourself.

There will always be things that you could have done better. Accept that you will make mistakes in life, and whenever possible, fail forward. You have the opportunity to correct your course and recognize that, if something in your life doesn't work, you can make adjustments. You don't have to redo everything. Try something new and learn from what happens.

Truth in Wisdom

What I've experienced to be true is that my thoughts—whether positive or negative—will influence my day. My thoughts cause me to rise and meet my goals or to descend and procrastinate till tomorrow. My intention is to avoid making excuses, and I work to be accountable for the effects that I have on others. My mistakes no longer hold me back—they push me forward each day toward a healthier future. As I continue to build on my faith, I appreciate the path that God lays in front of me. I progress with every act of service, every single prayer, every teardrop, every kind word. My unwavering faith opens my world to create, to explore fruitful ideas, and eventually to believe my dreams into existence.

In Matthew 17:20 (NIV), Jesus replies to an inquiry about why one is unable to do certain things, "Because you have so little faith. Truly I tell you, if you have faith as small as a mustard seed, you can say to this mountain, 'Move from here to there,' and it will move. Nothing will be impossible for you.'"

Nothing—how impactful and absolute.

As I move faithfully toward an intentional desire without any indication that it will happen—believing in the unseen—doors open and opportunities always show up. I center myself and pray to God that what I seek will eventually transpire. If I didn't have my faith, I don't know if I would have the courage to take as many chances as I do. It's scary to make a move when you don't know if you're making the right choice. I meditate and ruminate on the feelings of my heart, and I pray that I'm following the right path. I ask God to hold me and protect me on my journey.

My unwavering faith allows me to maintain consistent and intentional forward motion. Even if the progress isn't apparent, I put my trust in God, and I keep moving ahead day by day. I tend to my faith, and I put it in the forefront of my mind. Without that belief and trust, I can slip into a place of worry; it leads me to feel stuck, and the uneasiness robs my time.

There are incremental changes we make that allow us to maintain our forward direction. We don't have to reach our goals in a week or a month. Maintain your focus and commit to faith. Even if that forward movement is the size of a mustard seed, it's still progress.

There will be times when your goals will feel unreachable; even so, concentrate on your faith and keep going. You will need to course correct and steer your ship; that's assured. But keep moving toward the star you've chosen. Maintain your will and your desire, and trust in the certainty that God will help you make your dreams come true.

Trust in Action

Take fifteen minutes each day this month, either in the morning or at the end of the day. If you are a morning person, this exercise will help you wake up to a fresh new start, and if you're an evening person, it will help you unwind.

During this time, let go of the mistakes you've made that continue to hold you back and impede your growth. It doesn't matter how big or small the mistake is. Maybe you spoke harshly to a friend, and this is still troubling you, even if the other person has forgotten about it. Maybe you did a poor job on a group project at work, and you feel that you let your colleagues down. Acknowledge these mistakes and release them so that you can progress and learn from them.

Whenever possible, make a practice of apologizing directly to the people you've hurt. You can take them out for a meal, call them on the phone, write them a letter, or however you wish to communicate. Clear your conscience of your mistakes and move forward. There may be some people you want to apologize to but you're unable to communicate with them. Perhaps they've passed on or you've lost touch with them, or possibly you're no longer on speaking terms. In this case, write them a letter explaining why you're sorry for your actions, put the letter in a safe place, and then give yourself permission to release this burden. Allow yourself to feel the lightness of forgiveness, both for yourself and for the other person.

An important part of taking accountability is owning up to what you've done while also recognizing your humanity. Making mistakes is at the very core of what it is to be human. When you acknowledge what you've done wrong, you give the other person the chance to forgive; and in mending that rift, you both have the opportunity to become better people.

Find a quiet space where you will not be interrupted and unburden yourself from the tension of guilt and blame. Have a good cry, go for a run, practice yoga, exercise or whatever helps you. By the end of the month, you should feel lighter, gentler, and more accepting of yourself and others. Do your best to forgive yourself quickly. Resist the habit of clinging to the past, and your tomorrows will open doors that you could never imagine.

Visual Belief

Mistakes allow us to grow and teach us how to become more competent and confident as we progress in our lives. Perfection doesn't exist—open yourself to the humility and wonder of personal development. When the responsibility for apologizing or forgiving comes to you, ask God to allow you to grow from this. When given the opportunity, why not learn from it immediately? Why take years if you don't have to? Give thanks for the knowledge gained from slip-ups and blunders, and practice leniency and compassion. Ask God and the universe for forgiveness and forgive others swiftly and humbly.

Close your eyes and imagine yourself opening to the strength of vulnerability. Allow the regret and anger you've armored yourself with all these years to disperse like dandelions in the wind. Don't focus or wallow in your pain. We're each our own worst critic, and it's not healthy to live in a state of remorse. If you attack yourself, you'll become stuck and unable to move forward. See your pain, acknowledge it, and then let it go. Forgive yourself and others and shift your gaze to your new direction in life. What do you want to come to fruition? Practice patience with yourself and be gentle. Open yourself to the inner freedom that comes from kindness and compassion.

Recognize

If you find yourself stuck and unable to move forward, recognize that you will manifest inner freedom when you end your resistance to failure. When you try to keep yourself safe from loss, you will only make yourself small and limited. However, if you free your mind and open yourself to the possibility of failing, you will generate greater progress and success. To create change within, your mindset must yield and change. The more you feel free to fail, the easier it is to succeed. Peaceful surrender and unwavering faith are your connecting links to inner freedom.

We all go through difficulties in life. We experience the trauma of heartbreak and pain. Don't sugarcoat it, because when you are authentic, that is when you grow. That is when you will meet amazing people who have also faced similar challenges and emerged even stronger on the other side. These are the people who will celebrate you and hold you up, and you will be there to cheer them on as well. Life is so much more fulfilling and grounding when you acknowledge the pain and allow yourself to grow more powerful because of it.

True Story of Unwavering Faith

My inner freedom has come from accepting the blessing of singlehood. I don't have to belong to someone in order to be happy. I know the beauty that comes from understanding that I don't need to define myself by my relationship with another. I could have remained married—unhappy, but still married, with all the social benefits that marriage brings. However, I knew that I needed to let go and refuse the unacceptable no matter the fear.

Inner freedom comes from being truthful and forgiving; it comes from loving yourself enough to give yourself what you need to thrive. Ending a toxic relationship allowed me to form many more healthy relationships. It's easy to become depleted by people who want to steal your light and drain your energy. I had to protect my autonomy and uphold my accountability. Empowering myself—empowers others when you stand up for yourself and assert what you need.

My journey to my authentic self, I am certain, will be a lifetime process. It has been joyful, emotionally exhausting, filled with raw sorrow, loving, heartbreaking, revealing, and transformative. It seemed that, for many years, the long way was my only route; however, I had a burning desire for change and revelation. I was not sure what to expect, but I knew I needed to grow in order to set myself free. I innately understood that I needed to shed my old skin in order to move forward. I stood transfixed, eager, and excited to learn more about my life's purpose. How can I free myself from the fear of living my best life?

I prayed and honed my desire for inner direction and freedom. I opened myself to the answers that came to me peacefully. I separated myself from toxic love relationships, moved on from unfulfilling friendships, and searched for employment that I found satisfying. I wanted to seek a healthy balance in my life, and that meant loving and honoring myself. I stretched out my arms to welcome the unknown. I outgrew my old shell, and I embraced my longing for a new life.

It takes courage to follow your inner freedom. You will be tested many times through this process of shedding. You may experience challenges, change your career, move to a different city; whatever the trial may be, take the leap of freedom. Design your years going forward around the kind of life you desire to experience. No longer settle for crumbs; live in joy and discover what inner freedom truly feels like.

In him and through faith in him we may approach
God with freedom and confidence.
—Ephesians 3:12, NIV

Songs for Inner Freedom

Begin your journey to inner freedom with thankfulness and appreciation. Here is a powerful song of faith, along with an instrumental selection and two secular hits to help you focus as you journal:

- o *Song of faith*
  - – "Fearless" by Jasmine Murray
- o *Instrumental music*
  - – "Everdream" by Epic Soul Factory
- o *Secular songs*
  - – "Brand New Me" by Alicia Keys
  - – "Level Up" by Ciara

Journaling for Inner Freedom

I believe and receive inner freedom with unwavering faith and envision my life today as:

_____

_____

_____

_____

_____

_____

Jeannie Burgos

There are no guarantees in life; however, having unwavering faith in inner freedom allows you to love more deeply and connect more intimately. Discover yourself. Go deep and release what has to be put to rest. Focus on your heartfelt thoughts for good and what you desire to experience. Relationships with family, friends, and romantic partners will flourish when you release the need to please and, instead, focus on what makes you healthy and happy. Meditate on forgiveness for yourself and those who have hurt you, soak up the moment, and look to the future. Choose your path, see your new tomorrow, and keep your faith in the forefront.

Never allow negative talk to keep you from your guided path.
—Jeannie Burgos

Poem for Inner Freedom

Inner freedom allows you to express what your heart longs to sing
By deciding to overcome and learn from the challenge's life brings.
Build with faith and courage, and spread your luminous wings
As you soar through the darkest times and into a new spring.

Inner freedom is light, warm, and easy.
It's not a fight, a struggle, or obscurity
But a knowing—an insight—an intimacy
With where you are going—approaching—simplicity.

Inner freedom liberates from negativity and surrenders your soul.
It delivers the very gift you desire most of all.
It releases you from disapproval and demolishes your walls.
No matter the obstacles—surrender and decide to win,
For inner freedom is the gift that always lies within.

Photo by Jeannie Burgos

CHAPTER 3

March: Unconditional Love

If I have the gift of prophecy and can fathom all mysteries
and all knowledge, and if I have a faith that can move
mountains, but do not have love, I am nothing.
—1 Corinthians 13:2, NIV

For the Month of March

There is no need to worry, for everything is working out perfectly in the design of your life. As you become more intentional in creating your life as you want to live it, you will find that it's vital to practice unconditional love. Allow yourself some sacred time to reconnect with your inner peace, and you'll notice that serenity will follow. Your journey has not stopped because of delays, hindrances, or holdups. For if you take the time to love yourself and reconnect with your soul, you will see how things will move in the direction of your desires.

Unconditional love for yourself is a dreamlike sensation and a calm comprehension that positive change is taking place. Any situation at hand will work for your betterment. Be not confused or angry about how things are proceeding, even if things have not gone your way recently. Right now, it's up to you to be the change you seek. Once you give to yourself what you want most, which is love, all that is good will follow.

Take time to reconnect with yourself from a place of love and acceptance. If you allow other people's opinions to cloud your self-perception, you may get swept up in the turmoil of self-doubt. Embody unconditional love and open yourself to self-acceptance, and you will discover a profound inner peace.

Learning to have unconditional love for yourself is the practice for March; however, it should not be limited to only one month. The beautiful thing about self-love is that, once you get a taste, you will realize that one month isn't enough. It's a lesson that you'll want to carry with you for all the days of your life. Take time for yourself and allow your heart to be full. Understand that you cannot pour from an empty cup. If you pour for everyone else first and only leave a few drops for yourself, you will not be able to sustainably help others. If you fill your own heart with love, you won't feel drained or like you have nothing left to offer. You will have an overflow of love, and you can give that abundance to the people in your life who matter most.

To Achieve Unconditional Love through Unwavering Faith

The best way to tame the struggles outside of you is through the gift of gently and patiently loving yourself. Cherish yourself enough to require more of yourself and for yourself. You are not being selfish; rather, you are making a declaration that you matter in the equation of your life.

An important part of practicing unconditional love for yourself is recognizing that love is an intentional action. On the flip side, realize that not loving yourself is also an intentional act. It's a habit that we all get into at some point during our lives. Possibly, as little children, before we first encountered the belief that loving oneself wasn't "cool," self-love was a natural state. Then those innocent little bubbles were popped. Perhaps we endured bullying from our peers; we witnessed our parents going through a bitter divorce; we suffered the heartache of breaking up with our first love. Slowly and insidiously, we began the practice of self-doubt. These kinds of events inevitably detour us to start looking for love, acceptance, and validation from other people, especially those we perceive as superior. As we lose ourselves, we give more and more in the hopes that this will make us deserving of affection. Eventually, we give so much of ourselves that we find it hard to see the value and worth that we innately possess.

Giving yourself unconditional love is the antidote to insecurity and self-doubt. Accept yourself in all your facets and beauty and show the people in your life how you want to be treated and loved. An essential part of the practice of self-love is establishing boundaries and expectations with others. Many of us fall into a pattern of giving everything and then feeling depleted. You cannot blame those who unknowingly infringe on your unstated borders. You must set clear limits with people. Let them know, "This is what I have to give," and be okay with it. Remember, you cannot give what you don't have.

It is up to you to decide when you need to give yourself some healthy distance from certain people so that you can recoup your energy and avoid becoming derailed. It can be as simple as taking a few minutes to breathe and center yourself before you answer an email or rescheduling a meeting with someone to a day that won't take as much of your stamina. When you practice self-love and set boundaries out of respect for yourself and others, you will find that you no longer need to respond negatively to get people to acknowledge your limited resources. You won't feel bitter and resentful that people don't seem to recognize how much you are doing for them. When you say "yes" all the time, you will be inundated by requests and favors that ultimately leave you empty. People will assume you have plentiful resources, and they will continue to ask for more and more until you set your limit.

Learning to say, "I cannot," "no," "perhaps next time," "let me check my schedule," and "regrettably, I'm not available," will free you up to what you desire to say *yes* to. Learning the practice of unconditional self-love is acknowledging that you are not going to please everyone. You are still worthy of love. Come back to yourself and your needs and refill your cup to overflow.

Thought

The only way anyone can make you feel inferior is if you accept it as true. Take a moment to recall an occasion when a person made a demeaning comment about you. What was your immediate reaction? Did you believe it and take it to heart, or did you simply let it go and not allow those negative words to penetrate? When others utter disapproval or criticism, take a moment to breathe. Don't respond critically; instead, open your heart so you may feel that they are merely expressing their own thoughts and advice.

We have all had people criticize and disparage us. Sometimes their criticism is obvious, and sometimes it's not. It may take a while to realize that you have internalized another person's censure. People who devalue either cunningly or blatantly do so because it has been allowed in the past, and they believe they can continue to get away with it. Be aware, reject their negativity, and set boundaries.

Toxic people will often play on your self-doubt—the subconscious, negative thoughts that are part of your deepest insecurities. If you allow multiple people to take advantage of you in this way, recognize that this may be a pattern in your life. In this case, it is even more crucial to practice self-love. Love yourself fully and value your feelings, even if you must walk away to set a loving boundary.

Sometimes it helps to consider, *Would I allow this treatment to go on if I saw it happening to someone I deeply care about? Would I speak up?* More than likely, you would speak up. Even if it were uncomfortable, you would talk to your loved one and let them know that the way they are being treated isn't okay. You would most likely help him or her stand up for themselves and encourage separation from the situation.

As you grow and become more enlightened, there will be people who will not grow with you. They may leave you when you become more self-assured. With time and wisdom, however, you will be thankful for their absence. Ask God, "If they are not here for good, then please fade them out of my life." As painful as it can sometimes be to lose someone who's been part of your life, you may experience a lighter and less chaotic existence without someone treating you in a way that diminishes you. By practicing self-love and setting boundaries, you demonstrate yourself to be an individual with integrity and fearlessness.

Truth in Wisdom

What I've experienced to be true is that loving myself with high regard is the secret to protecting myself from disapproval and criticism. I take the time to work on me and express gratitude for all that shows up, even the unfavorable. This practice has strengthened my faith and has given me the power to rise above when life throws a wrench in my plans. I know that God is the one in control, and I must surrender to Him in trust.

This understanding has taken time. I still trip, make mistakes, and need mental health days; however, no matter the circumstances, I still take time to regroup and reenergize myself. I practice gratitude and thankfulness for all that I have in my life, including the disadvantageous—I have learned not to take anything for granted. I reaffirm the love I feel for myself and those around me, and I let go of negativity. If I focus my attention on the disapproval from others, I will receive more negativity in quick succession. Unwarranted judgments from other people multiply, my energy drops further, and it becomes a downward spiral.

As I've worked to become aware of my patterns, I'm able to recognize when I need to take some loving time for myself. It can be a walk around the block, a dance break in the living room, or an hour at the gym to sweat the stress away. I take deep breaths and clear my mind. I come back refreshed; I deal with whatever comes my way; and I approach it from a place of love.

Be gentle with yourself and practice forgiveness when you notice yourself engaging in negative self-talk. Everybody has times when they fall back on old habits. Each time you find yourself straying from the path of self-acceptance, take a break to pray and meditate. Engage in practices that uplift you—listen to inspirational music, talk to a dear friend, volunteer for a good cause. Elevate your mood, and you will notice your energy rise. Welcome yourself back with the understanding that this is another opportunity to practice self-love.

Trust in Action

Take thirty minutes every day this month. Look into a mirror and allow God's love to seep into your soul. Don't merely look at your image; look into your eyes—your essence, your spirit, your soul. Acknowledge yourself through the eyes of unconditional love. That is how God sees you. His love is boundless. God cherishes and accepts you exactly as you are, no matter what. When you look in the mirror, think to yourself, *I love myself as God does. I matter to God, and I matter to me.*

Repeat these positive affirmations and embody each word: "I am good. I am kind. I am loving. I am wonderful. I am beautiful. I am special. I am successful. I am generous. I am gracious. I am loved. I am light. I am precious. I am treasured. I am trustworthy. I am courageous. I am unique. I am prosperous. I am enough." Add in whatever it is that you intend and need to hear. Repeat these constructive declarations often—especially when obstacles arise. Post-it notes are great for this—write your affirmations on them, stick them to your mirror, and read them every time you look at yourself.

When experiencing negative emotions, either within or from other people, it's important to find a way to believe in the goodness that resides within you. Little by little, you'll feel more powerful and confident. When experiencing negative emotions, either within or from other people, it's important to find a way to believe in the goodness that resides within you. Little by little, you'll feel more powerful and confident.

If you notice negative attributes about yourself that you want to change, then change them kindly and with love. You are with you every second of every day. Practice what you want to receive—unconditional love. It's not something that can be automated; it's a conscious daily choice.

When self-doubt creeps in, disrupt your negative thoughts by internally saying, *Stop.* Tell yourself, *I love myself enough to silence this negative self-talk; it is not part of me.* Recognize the negativity for what it is and establish your own authentic and strong inner voice. State what you want to personify and believe in this manifestation of self with all your heart. Soon, you will have grown to a point where you won't acknowledge anything less than unconditional love and acceptance.

Visual Belief

Fill your cup to overflow and experience the reward of giving in abundance to those you love. As you learn to love yourself, you will attract love from others, because you attract who you are. You'll be amazed at the positive energy you inspire in others when you give positive energy to yourself. As you allow love and light to come in, the people who are drawn to your inner circle will be filled with light as well. You will brighten each other's days and change one another's outlook on life.

When I go to a concert, event, or a show, I will often buy two tickets and invite a friend or family member who wouldn't be able to go otherwise. I pray to God, and ask Him to show me who would enjoy sharing the experience with me. Maybe someone is overwhelmed at work, needs a break from responsibilities at home, or financially can't afford to go. I know that going out and having a fun evening helps me tremendously, so I want to share some of that sweetness to help someone else relax and recharge.

Recognize

I have a saying that I like to repeat to myself: "My oxygen mask first." You have probably been on an airplane and heard the flight attendant say that, in the case of an emergency, you should put on your oxygen mask before assisting others. If you don't have your oxygen mask on, you can't help anyone else. This is an example of unconditional self-love. Take care of yourself first because you can't help anyone else if you can't breathe.

Give what you can without draining yourself dry. Show people what you want to receive. When you respond to crises with anger, guilt, and blame, that's the energy that will come back to you. When you express your needs in a loving way and give people your respect by trusting that they'll understand your limits, you will earn their love, respect, and trust in return.

True Story of Unwavering Faith

What is unconditional love? I describe it as loving without exception or expectation; it's loving yourself and others as you are, not as you want them to be. Unconditional love is pure, patient, forgiving, everlasting, protective, kind, devoted, gentle, fruitful, and generous.

My daughters first taught me the meaning of unconditional love. From the moment they were in my womb, they changed my life forever. My heart opened up like never before when I became a mother. I am so thankful to

God for the gift of motherhood. I understand how precious life is and what a gift it is to be a mother. We are not handed a manual to raise our children, and so we do the best we can. We hope they will see our hearts and feel the love that overflows for them. Every child offers a gift we must unwrap and appreciate. They wander and try to find their way. They challenge us and disobey. And as parents, we must love as God loves—unconditionally; with empathy, understanding, respect, positive regard and genuineness.

When you are gifted with a precious life, you will do anything to feed them, clothe them, give them a roof over their head, and even spoil them at times. The many milestones I've had with my daughters have been the best years of my life. Even through divorce, trials and tribulations, and raising them as a single parent, I am totally grateful. My daughters have taught me to love without expecting anything in return; however, what does return is love—love wrapped up with an overflow of goodness, closeness, and loyalty.

Remember that you are deserving of unconditional love, too. You are a soul that is loved by God despite your failures and mistakes. Embrace His love and seek Him. He will reassure you and your faith will become unwavering.

Beloved, let us love one another, for love comes from God.
Everyone who loves has been born of God and knows God.
—1 John 4:7, ESV

Songs for Unconditional Love

Begin your journey to unconditional love with self-reflection, forgiveness, and positive declarations. Here is a powerful song of faith, along with an instrumental selection and two secular hits to help you focus as you journal:

- o *Song of faith*
  - – "Fighting for Me" by Riley Clemmons
- o *Instrumental music*
  - – "A Thousand Years" by Christina Perri, piano/cello cover
- o *Secular songs*
  - – "Speechless" by Dan + Shay
  - – "Love Myself" by Hailee Steinfeld

Journaling for Unconditional Love

I believe and receive unconditional love with unwavering faith and envision my life today as:

_____

_____

_____

_____

_____

_____

_____

_____

_____

_____

_____

_____

_____

_____

_____

_____

_____

_____

_____

_____

_____

_____

_____

_____

Communicate your boundaries in a loving way. Many people don't mean to impose on your limits—they simply don't know where those limits are. They have been used to you giving and giving, and so naturally they ask again. When you pour from an overflowing cup, it becomes a beautiful give and take. State clearly what you have to offer and show that you are giving from your heart. Keep the rest for yourself, and the other person will feel blessed that they received this gift from you—the very best of you.

> *Quit making excuses as to "why me" and*
> *make allowances as to "yes me."*
> —Jeannie Burgos

Poem for Unconditional Love

Unconditional love is accepting and caring for one another
So we may come to see each other as sister and brother.
It is to quickly and gently forgive our neighbor
So our hearts may grow softer and bigger.

Unconditional love lifts our spirits when we are down
So we may inspire others to climb and sail through all bounds.
It helps us discover the compelling power within
So we may be the leading light for others to win.

How amazing to give without expectation?
To open your heart and soul and love with anticipation.
Unconditional love is belief, respect, trust, and grace
For all to obtain, to cherish, and to forever embrace.

Photo by Jeannie Burgos

CHAPTER 4
April: Forgiveness

Be kind to one another, tenderhearted, forgiving
one another, as God in Christ forgave you.
—Ephesians 4:32, ESV

For the Month of April

Understand that nearly everyone has been hurt by the actions or words of another. These wounds can leave you with lasting feelings of anger, bitterness, or even vengeance. However, if you don't practice forgiveness, you might be the one who pays most dearly. By embracing forgiveness, you can also embrace peace, hope, gratitude, and joy. Consider how forgiveness can lead you down the path of physical, emotional, and spiritual well-being. Forgive to live!

When you choose bitterness and resentment over forgiveness, the only person you hurt is yourself. Forgiveness is choosing to love yourself and to release the negative bonds that tie you to the other person. The more you hold onto what was, the more you give others the power to hurt you. Days turn into weeks and then months and even years, and throughout that time, you are weighed down by the heavy burden of the grudge you carry. Let go and understand that forgiveness is for yourself. You are closing the chapter on the book of that relationship.

When you forgive someone, you're not justifying the person's actions or making excuses for the harmful behavior. You're not saying that what they did was right or okay. You are choosing to let go of the emotions that bind you to them. You may be holding onto feelings of sadness and anger, and you are the one who is made ill. When you think of them, hear their voice, or see them in person, your feelings of resentment will bring up that past trauma again and again. So really, who is it hurting? Let go and understand that, by choosing forgiveness, you are choosing freedom.

To Achieve Forgiveness through Unwavering Faith

Forgiveness is a commitment to a process of change. As you let go of grudges, you'll no longer define your life by how you've been hurt. You might even find compassion and understanding for those who've harmed you.

There are people in your life who have wronged you and will never apologize for what they've done. Perhaps they've passed on or moved away, or perhaps they are still in your life but are too oblivious or prideful to acknowledge what they've done. Whatever the case may be, allow yourself to let go of the pain and anger you feel.

Generally, forgiveness is a decision to release resentment and thoughts of revenge. The act that hurt or betrayed you might always remain a part of your life, but forgiveness can lessen its grip on you and help you focus on other, more positive parts of your journey. Forgiveness can even lead to feelings of understanding, empathy, and compassion for the ones who hurt you. You will want to bottle the good that comes from forgiveness. It's an epiphany elixir.

Thought

When you forgive those who have harmed you, you soften your ego and liberate yourself to joy and happiness. Let compassion shelter your heart and allow forgiveness to come quickly and easily. Ask yourself, *"How may I offer forgiveness without expectation?"* If you forgive with strings attached, it defeats the intent of a wholehearted release of negativity. Contemplate and pray, *"How may I offer forgiveness with compassion and peaceful restoration of tarnished relationships?"* If reconciliation is not possible, I ask for healing of my heart and forgiveness for those who have infringed against me.

As you pray and meditate on forgiveness, imagine the other person in front of you and practice releasing the grudges you hold. Feelings will come into play. You may end up crying as you cleanse your heart and let go. Surrender to that catharsis. Imagine cutting the ties that bind you to the other person. Express what you have bottled up and been afraid to say so that healing may begin and heartache may end. If you see that person again, you will not have the same experience of being in your old conflict with the person. You will no longer feel like they are pulling the bandage off a fresh, open wound. No matter what they said or did or took from you, they will never again have that power over you. Forgive today so that you can let go of what happened yesterday. Allow yourself to see the other person with empathy. Remember, hurt people crush people. We are all imperfect and learning as we go. When you can see yourself in the shoes of the person who hurt you, it will be easier to forgive.

Practice putting what has happened to you in context. This is important for letting go of the emotions that bind you. Without excusing what the person has done, allow yourself to break those ties. Find the wisdom in that emotional release. So many people believe that, if we don't stay angry, we are silently condoning what the other person did. Learn to distinguish forgiving from excusing. You can acknowledge that what those who've hurt you did was wrong, and you can still let go of your anger, because anger will only compromise your health and prevent you from growing. Choose peace, gratitude, and joy, and look to the future.

As time goes on, try to find the lessons in what happened. This person came into your life to teach you something. Seek to understand what you can from this. Don't resent your past—learn from it. Expand your understanding and go within. It's essential to forgive yourself as well. Heal that part of yourself that feels guilty for allowing the other person to touch your soul and wound you so deeply. Forgiveness is everything. Otherwise, all you're doing is shadowboxing with someone in your memory, and reliving history over and over again.

Truth in Wisdom

What I have experienced to be true is that, when I free myself from old defeating stories such as *"Why did they hurt me? They don't deserve my forgiveness. I will never speak to them again!"*; I embrace the reward of letting go and allowing forgiveness to seep in. Forgiving is going within that sacred place called peace. When you yield and release the unnecessary stress from holding onto resentment and bitterness, you align yourself to bigger and greater things that are waiting to be revealed.

While it's important to practice forgiveness and understanding, it's also important to accept that some people will never be able to come back into your life. If someone has been abusive to you, stand strong and know that you will not condone that kind of treatment again. Be clear that you are choosing forgiveness because forward is where you want to go.

The other person may have evolved, or maybe they haven't. But regardless of someone else's journey, it is your responsibility to move toward a place of healing. Hatred only keeps the dynamic going between you and your perception of the other person. You become a prisoner to your mental image of them. This is especially true when the person has passed on. You're maintaining your righteous anger at a memory. Let go of that negativity and strive for a place of balance.

Trust in Action

Take thirty minutes each day this month and write a letter to those you want to forgive. These letters will be for your eyes only. Writing them will allow you to release the tension, pain, and sorrow you carry. You will notice the weight of anger lifting and becoming lighter with time.

You may find it cathartic to write these letters longhand, or you may prefer to type them on your computer. Write from your heart so that you may release the tension you hold within. Put the core essence of what you feel on paper. Take time for yourself—cry, shout, exercise, create, sing, do whatever you need to do to free the feelings of hurt. Then save the letter, either on your computer or in a physical location. Do not send it. It can be useful to read these letters several months later and see how differently you feel then. Release frustration, stress, and anger, and give it up to God to handle. Letting go and letting God opens your heart to receive wisdom, growth, and gratitude.

Visual Belief

Envision yourself forgiving someone in your life who you believe does not deserve it. Picture them receiving your forgiveness with a humble and loving demeanor and feel how liberating it is to let go of the anchor of bitterness. Start with one person who has wronged you who you haven't spoken to for a while. Visualize the person accepting your forgiveness and feeling true remorse for their actions. Allow their love to wash over you.

I know that forgiveness is a heavy topic. You may have tried to avoid it. You might even have tried to convince yourself that you are fine holding onto a grudge. This exercise will help you release resentment. Visualize a person you once loved. You cared about the person deeply, but your relationship turned sour, and your paths needed to diverge. Maybe you haven't seen each other for months or even years. Now, visualize that you encounter the person in public one day. Imagine the release you will feel when you're able to face your long-lost friend or the person whose memory tormented you without anger or fear and fully forgive them for their wrongdoings. Embrace them with love and kindness in your heart and breathe in peacefulness.

Now direct your forgiveness to yourself. Forgive yourself for staying with the person past the point when things became toxic. At the end of the day, we all have that somebody. We've all experienced holding onto grudges that harm us. Imagine how cleansing it will be when you cut the cords of pain and anger that bind you to those who've hurt you and move forward in your life.

If you want, this exercise can be the start of you picking up the phone or sending an email. Maybe you want to invite the person to catch up with you and talk. You may be surprised. They might have been waiting for you to reach out to them. Perhaps they've wanted to find closure, but they've been too embarrassed or ashamed to get in touch with you.

If you aren't ready or able to reach out to them in person, visualize yourself forgiving them and letting them go. This is especially important if neither of you wish to be in contact or if the other person has passed on. This can transform the most tumultuous relationships into peaceful expressions of love. Even if you think you will never be able to forgive the other person, consider that you can learn from the pain and, ultimately, release it. It can be as simple as an email sent without expectation of reply. You might never speak to them again, but composing a statement of forgiveness to them, even indirectly, can help bring closure. Allow yourself that release, no matter how awkward or uncomfortable it might feel in the moment. With time, you will discover that forgiveness is not about the other person at all; it is ultimately about loving and cherishing yourself.

Recognize

Recognize that forgiveness is the key to finding peace within. We relinquish the hold of resentment when we forgive. We waste so much time and energy harboring feelings of anger, bitterness, and hatred. When you let go and let God, the healing begins.

Be mindful that forgiveness and compassion are vital and possible, even in the most difficult circumstances. Pay attention to who may be watching you practice forgiveness, especially children. Be the example you desire your children and love ones to emulate.

True Story of Unwavering Faith

I chose to open myself to forgiveness because I no longer wanted to live with resentment burdening my soul. Too often, we get so stuck in our own pain and ego that we miss out on that healing journey. As I forgive, it releases my soul from the chained memories that used to keep me prisoner. It offers healing, restoration, and confidence to go to someone and tell them that no matter what they did in the past, you want to move forward and forgive them.

I have wholeheartedly forgiven many times, and I have asked for forgiveness of those I have unintentionally hurt. It has been a gift to experience genuine kindness for one another and to let go of the stress of bitterness through empathy and compassion. I've witnessed love overcoming hatred and fear, and I've seen benevolence melting away past offenses.

Life has brought me to my knees with sorrow and pain, but from that place of humbleness, I have surrendered with a new heart and fresh eyes to see that I am forgiven by God. Without forgiveness, I wouldn't be the mother, sister, daughter, and friend I am today. I have chosen to heal and love unconditionally, and because of that decision, I understand the beauty of forgiveness. I am forever grateful for this peace and harmony that I feel today.

Life is not black and white; it is colorful, messy, and beautiful. Decide not to carry anger and animosity any longer—the burden of that grudge ends with you. Forgiveness is how we stop the pain within and begin to heal. Learn to forgive completely, with all flaws and imperfections because we are all flawed and imperfect. No regrets.

> *And when you stand praying, if you hold anything against anyone,*
> *forgive them, so that your Father in heaven may forgive you your sins.*
> —Mark 11:25, NIV

Songs for Forgiveness

Begin your journey to forgiveness with patience, compassion, and encouraging statements. Here is a powerful song of faith, along with an instrumental selection and two secular hits to help you focus as you journal:

- o *Song of faith*
    - – "Peace Be Still" by Hope Darst
- o *Instrumental music*
    - – "Let the Past be the Past" by Walter Bergmann
- o *Secular songs*
    - – "Fighter" by Christina Aguilera
    - – "Blank Page" by Christina Aguilera

Journaling for Forgiveness

I believe and receive forgiveness with unwavering faith and envision my life today as:

_____

_____

_____

_____

_____

_____

Teach by example. If you represent a noble and kind heart, and demonstrate that we are all deserving of love, others will in turn witness how to forgive. Peace is built on decisions we make and actions we take. Your heart will be freer, lighter, and safer because you choose to surrender with swiftness, gratitude, and compassion.

> *All lessons in life are lessons of love. Be your own*
> *therapist—go within and do the work.*
> —Jeannie Burgos

Poem for Forgiveness

Forgive despite what your ego echoes to attest.
Forgive yourself and put past guilt and shame to rest.
Keep your heart open to self-love; that is the test,
For love protects us from those we rightly mistrust.

To grow from that which we think we can't forgive
Is to let go and begin to truly live.
Forgive those who have wronged you without delay;
Make way for a new start, a new self, a new day.

Allow your heart to heal from the heavy load of many years.
Take a chance and forgive those who have surfaced insincere.
Soften your soul, and embrace the peace without fear.
And forgive yourself and you will rise and shine like a star my dear.

Photo by Jeannie Burgos

CHAPTER 5

May: Gratitude

Devote yourselves to prayer, being watchful and thankful.
—Colossians 4:2, NIV

For the Month of May

If you want more happiness, joy, energy, love, and kindness in your life, then gratitude is an essential quality to cultivate. It is a fullness of heart that moves us from limitation and fear to expansion and love. When we enter a state of appreciation, our ego moves out of the way and we connect with our soul—our innate being.

Gratitude brings our attention to the present moment, the space where miracles can unfold. The deeper our appreciation, the more we see with the eyes of the soul, and the more our life flows in harmony with the creative power of the universe.

Make it your way of life to practice gratitude for all things, great and small. Be grateful for my body and your health, for without your health, you have nothing. Be grateful for your relationships with family, friends, and colleagues. Be grateful for your career and the opportunities that it has given you. Be grateful for the holidays and all the times you get to be in the company of your loved ones. Be grateful for your children and the joy they bring into your life. Practice gratitude statements every single day. Gratitude is a powerful state that leads directly to joy and prosperity. The more you are thankful for the things that come into your life, the more things to be grateful for.

To Achieve Gratitude through Unwavering Faith

If you want to experience greater levels of happiness, fulfillment, and well-being, it's essential to keep a gratitude journal. Journaling allows you to go within and express what you appreciate and value in your life. In turn, like a boomerang, goodness and appreciation will come back to you. Keep your journal current and fresh to what is happening today. If you wish to, you can rewrite a pleasant experience from your past or state something that you are looking forward to in the future; however, write from the perspective of the present moment. Like life, gratitude happens in the present tense.

Be grateful for the little and big things that arise in your life, moment by moment—basking in the sun, listening to your favorite songs, getting together with a good friend, taking time to pray or meditate. What's important is that you consistently and consciously focus your mind on your blessings.

Commit to writing in your gratitude journal every day—what you put your attention to will expand in your life. By offering appreciation for all the goodness that you experience, you invite more and more of what you desire. Look for the miracles that appear daily, and gratitude will become your new reality.

So often when someone asks us what we are grateful for, we get stuck trying to come up with an example that is huge, magnificent, or once-in-a-lifetime, and we end up discounting all the instances of everyday gratitude that are easily within our reach. Seek out experiences where you can be undeniably thankful. Some people might call these "simple" things, like the gratitude you feel when you see May flowers beginning to blossom, transforming the landscape into an abundance of color. I prefer to think of these as pure experiences, for there is nothing simple about them. Indeed, they are incredibly profound and a gift to acknowledge and be grateful for.

Thought

To live in gratitude is to live in appreciation and kindness. It is a state of joy—an expression of the heart that is generous and open to consideration for others. If you make a daily decision to express thankfulness in all parts of your life, you will notice a shift that is contagious and benevolent.

Ask yourself, *"How may I receive and offer gratitude on a regular basis?"* As you make gratitude practice a must and place it in the forefront of your day, you will experience happiness, joy, and appreciation that comes directly from God. Gratitude is not just being polite or cordial; it is an expression of loving and caring connection. Contemplate with, *"May I offer and experience gratitude in the highest form so I may touch souls with my thoughts, words, and actions, lovingly and anonymously."*

It is your responsibility to maintain a positive outlook. To set yourself up for success, it's important to cultivate a mental state of seeing the cup as half full instead of half empty. Make plans to enjoy today, and your hours will be full of beauty and abundance.

How do you remain in this state when life is happening all around you? It starts with the practice of everyday appreciation and enthusiasm follows. It's a shift in attention. Focus on the things that bring you delight and wonder; savor with emphasis. Doing this regularly allows the practice to become second nature. It's not something that you should try to force. It is a flow not a force. You can simply tap into that state whenever you want. Make it a part of your everyday routine and it will become a fruitful commitment.

Truth in Wisdom

What I have experienced to be true is that the more I open myself to gratitude, the more gracious and appreciative I become. Gratitude fulfills me and connects me to people on all levels—family-wise, socially, and professionally.

I have discovered what it is to be in full gratitude. It is to verbalize my thankfulness, to be thoughtful with my gestures, and to mindfully brighten someone's day. Gratitude connects me to the genuine bond of friendship. It is the ability to display compassion and to acknowledge without expectation—a surprise gift, a dinner with a friend, a letter of admiration.

I often practice "gratitude echo," where I express appreciation for all the things that bring me joy in my current environment and repeat it. Try this yourself. Start by listing what you immediately connect with and are grateful for and you'll tap into an abundance mindset. Soon, gratitude will become natural and automatic. People will start noticing your new outlook, and they will be drawn to you. Being in a state of grateful openness allows you to embody an inherently charismatic energy. Like draws like, and you will gather other kindred spirits who are following the same path of joy and prosperity.

Trust in Action

Take thirty minutes each day this week and express gratitude by writing notes to those you are grateful for. This will offer thirty-one messages to loved ones, children, significant others, relatives, coworkers, friends, and all those who have changed your life. Some of these people may not even be aware of the impact they have had on you over the years.

If you are not able to come up with thirty-one people, include the waitress who usually serves you at the diner, the bus driver who makes sure you arrive safely, the hairdresser who takes you in at the last minute, the doorman who holds the door and handles your bags, the teller who greets you with a smile.

These letters should be handwritten—writing by hand shows heart and thoughtfulness, and most of all, it offers a personalized gift from you to the receiver.

An equally profound exercise is to write thank you letters to yourself. See yourself as a person who deserves your gratitude. Take the time to thank yourself for having the courage to persevere—you have taken risks, dared to be bold, and pulled through even though the journey has been hard. Acknowledge the times when you had to take a step back, cry on someone's shoulder, and regroup. Thank yourself for getting back up after each fall and tell yourself how proud you are that you've kept moving forward through all the highs and lows.

After you finish writing, put each letter in an envelope and seal it. You can even address the envelopes and send them to yourself. Open each packet and read your letters, allowing your words to yourself to permeate into your soul. Then tuck the letters away in a place where you can come back and read them again. Read them when you need an infusion of courage or when you have reached a new milestone toward your goal. Allow your letters to reinforce your resolve and show that you deserve to accomplish your dreams and appreciate the journey to come.

Visual Belief

Envision yourself being grateful for *everything*. See yourself as more trusting, forgiving, and considerate. Kindness strengthens and improves all your relationships. See yourself as open, sociable, and empathic to others on a deeper level. Observe others and be thankful for the little things they do for you.

Visualize where you want to go in life and what you want to experience along the way. Be grateful that you can rise to life's challenges. God gives you the strength to get back up when you've been knocked down; you continue to move forward, even through hardship and loss. Acknowledge and be thankful for both the favorable and the unfavorable. Celebrate your struggles and all the times that you've fought to succeed. Praise yourself for the fact that you have kept going, even when you wanted to quit.

Be thankful for everyone in your life who has helped move you closer to your goals. You have met many kindred souls who have stuck by your side and guided you. Even give thanks to the people who have doubted you the most. The people who dare you to fail are sometimes your biggest motivators, because they push you to stand up for yourself and improve day after day. Be grateful for them all.

Picture five people who you see as a blessing in your life. Think of ways to thank each of them—surprising them with a picnic outdoors, picking up some flowers and arranging them yourself, writing them a touching letter of gratitude, or giving them a gift of appreciation. As you focus on their happiness, the love you feel seeps over and fills your cup as well.

Recognize

To have unwavering faith in gratitude is to firmly believe that God and the universe (depending on your belief) will give you what you want when you ask for it. Become aware of the good things that happen to you and don't take them for granted. This mindset opens you to a state of kindness and appreciation that will become your standard.

Each day this month, ask yourself, *"Whom may I inspire today? Whom may I bring happiness today? Whom may I give comfort and deep peace today? Whom may I bless today?"* Meditate on these questions and take a few moments to consciously focus your mind on your loyalties.

Thankfulness is a feeling and gratefulness is an action—a demonstration of kindness and appreciation. Be thoughtful and compassionate, become a more active listener, connect and be attentive to those who need you, and offer support during the hard times. All these actions open your heart and show that you care.

Count your blessings daily. We live such busy lives and forget that we will never be as young as we are today, so give thanks for another day to live life fully and joyfully.

True Story of Unwavering Faith

I practice gratitude daily, even if it's for a few minutes at a time. I like to practice gratitude in motion. When I am on my way to work, getting ready for the gym, cooking a meal for the family, or taking a vacation with friends, I make it a priority to give thanks for the daily blessings—big or small. Having gratitude in the forefront of my day uplifts and inspires my soul, and my attitude becomes contagious. I see it affect those I interact with, which makes me celebrate even more.

Gratitude is embedded in my heart. It has opened my eyes and enriched my essence. It has changed my life in ways that I once could only have imagined. It's easy to be grateful for the accomplishments, good breaks, loving relationships, and promotions achieved; however, I have found true gratitude in the lessons I've learned from the hardships, breakups, loneliness, and financial instability I've experienced. These challenges have brought me into a closer relationship with God.

In my younger years, fear kept me immobilized, stagnant, and constricted by limiting beliefs. Slowly, I came to understand that gratitude holds the key to transforming my existence with peace, light, harmony, and joy. I also realized the importance of being forgiving and gentle with myself. We all make mistakes and have seasons of regret. I learned to pause, regroup, and surrender. God has been with me all along, willing me to thrive and not give up; to be still and trust what is to come. I hold peace as the gift that it is and allow it to direct me forward and favored.

I am grateful every day, even when events do not fall into place as I wish. When I am faced with obstacles, I ask God, *"What can I learn from this? How can I grow from this challenge? What changes must I make?"* I take the time to be still and at peace and usually get my answers on how to proceed.

I am certain that, no matter what may come, if dealt from a place of gratitude, clarity, awareness and peace will be your guide. Learn to trust and let go, observe a multitude of blessings show up in your life. You will become wiser with every stumble because each time is an opportunity to come back to yourself and reinforce your faith.

> *All this is for your benefit, so that the grace that is reaching more and more people may cause thanksgiving to overflow to the glory of God.*
> —2 Corinthians 4:15, NIV

Songs for Gratitude

Begin your journey to gratitude with appreciation, thankfulness, and inspiring statements. Here is a powerful song of faith, along with an instrumental selection and two secular hits to help you focus as you journal:

- o *Song of faith*
  - – "Make A Difference" by Danny Gokey
- o *Instrumental music*
  - – "Night Sky" by Tracey Cattaway
- o *Secular songs*
  - – "Win" by Brian McKnight
  - – "When I Pray for You" by Dan + Shay

Journaling for Gratitude

I believe and receive gratitude with unwavering faith and envision my life today as:

_____

_____

_____

_____

_____

_____

Jeannie Burgos

_____

_____

_____

_____

_____

_____

_____

_____

_____

_____

_____

_____

_____

_____

_____

_____

_____

Take thirty minutes each day this month and go on a gratitude walk. Think about whatever it is that you're thankful for. This is a particularly useful practice when you're feeling down or filled with stress and worry. Take that time and stroll in a park, wander around your neighborhood, or even walk in your office building. Consider the things that you are grateful for right now. Meditate on the nurturing relationships in your life, your body that allows you to experience health and well-being, your mind that helps you to understand yourself, your senses that can appreciate the blooming beauty of springtime, and your spiritual nature that connects you to the divine. Pay attention to everything you are seeing, hearing, feeling, smelling, and tasting, and see how many ways you can experience gratitude. Take time to pause, breathe, and be thankful that you're alive. This is a powerful way to shift your mood and open yourself to the flow of abundance that continually surrounds you.

> *Engrave kindness in people's hearts, and*
> *you will touch them forever.*
> —Jeannie Burgos

Poem for Gratitude

How powerful is the act of gratitude?
It will lift your state—it will change your outlook and your attitude.
Being grateful for today—for each moment can bring out the best of you.
You will notice blessings and favors appear in plentitude.

Gratitude is understanding how deep your love for another can be.
It is a deeper level—without expectation—in full beauty, you'll see,
When you extend your hand in friendship, acceptance, you'll receive.
You will feel safe, confident, brilliant, inspiring and free

Make gratitude a daily practice when you arise.
Learn to see the world through newly grateful eyes.
Gratitude is joy, fulfillment, truth, and peace with no disguise,
A priceless gift that makes your soul and heart grow wise.

Photo by Jeannie Burgos

CHAPTER 6

June: Courage

Be strong and courageous. Do not be afraid or terrified
because of them, for the Lord your God goes with
you; he will never leave you nor forsake you.
—Deuteronomy 31:6, NIV

For the Month of June

Courage is the act of being afraid and doing it anyway. When you give in to doubt, fear, and indecision, it holds you back from speaking your deepest truths, going for your boldest dreams, and sharing your unique gifts. Courage gives you the drive to say, *"I know things are hard, but my heart beats for more. I am made for more than mediocrity; I am going to pursue my dreams despite my fear."*

Go for what God has put you in this world to achieve. He gave each of us life for a reason, and that reason is for us to find out why we're here. It takes courage to go against the grain and pursue your life-altering aspirations. Even if you don't have someone to encourage you, do not be discouraged. You are building the muscles of bravery through the challenge. As that bold inner voice gets louder and louder, take the opportunity and make your move. If you don't, you may live a life of what-ifs. The Rolling Stones hit song "Time Waits For No One" is lyrical truth. To go through life without ever taking the chance to do what you truly desire is not living; it is merely existing.

Courage is the ingredient that allows us to say, *"I may be fearful, I may not have the answers on how to achieve what I want, but I am going to move forward despite my apprehension. Even if that means inching along, I will get there eventually."*

It takes courage to live each day with grace and be open to new possibilities. It's hard to transform yourself and your relationships or to decide that you don't want to give into mediocrity. It's an act of bravery when you quit a stable but dead-end job for an entrepreneurial pursuit or leave a familiar but unhappy marriage for happiness. It takes courage to pursue success and self-love.

Make conscious decisions to build your courage. Go skydiving, travel to different places, learn a new language, take a chance on love, pursue that dream job, buy your first home. You may experience, fear, anxiety, and worry rush forward to try and halt your goals; however, as you build the courage muscle, you will become more adventurous and less easily intimidated and disheartened. Once you make a practice of doing the things you're afraid of, you will realize that they aren't as painful or as hard as you thought they would be.

Believe in the power of letting the heart lead for good. Whatever may be calling you to pursue your dream, trust that God has you. Don't allow others to dissuade you from your life course, for God has put that dream inside of you. With courage and unwavering faith, you will find the drive to reach your goal and achieve your vision.

To Achieve Courage through Unwavering Faith

To achieve courage, you must dig deep within yourself and walk through the fear. When you feel apprehension and doubt creeping in, keep striding forward. Courage is an action; it isn't something that you get by asking for permission. Allow your actions to speak your intent.

Proceed unmoved when people downgrade or downplay your ambitions. People who try to discourage you often have regrets about dreams they never attempted to pursue or goals they gave up on too soon. If you need someone to speak to about your goals, pray in conversation to God. Listen to His divine whisper. He offers peace even through doubt.

When you experience failure, and we all do, don't let fear drive you to quit. Every time you fail, gather the courage to take another chance. We all have a choice between a memory book of adventures and a memory book of what-ifs. What is your choice?

Courage requires skin in the game. It takes being all in. You might have difficulties, hardships, and countless bills to pay, but don't give up on your God-given ideas. Dedicate time to your goals and build resources toward your vision. Each step you take will bring you closer to the finish line. Courage is an act of faith. You are trusting in God, knowing that He is directing your steps. He is showing you where to go and encouraging you to take a chance on yourself.

Thought

Courage is passion. It's fuel that powers our dreams. It opens doors and inspires us and others. Allow that passion to come through. Don't close yourself off because of what you've been through in the past, or what you've been told or conditioned to believe. Take that step and allow your God given talent to come through with courage. If you fail, then you took a chance—get up, dust yourself off, and try again.

If you don't allow yourself to follow your passion, how will you ever achieve it? Without courage, you will stay the same, you won't grow, and you won't experience transformation. You will miss opportunities of a lifetime if you don't allow yourself to walk through the fire and see what's on the other side.

Truth in Wisdom

What I've experienced to be true is that courage brings out the best in us. I've taken daring chances and have become a stronger, more dedicated, and more committed person. I now go that extra mile to accomplish things that I was afraid to do before.

Courage is the realization that you don't just exist; you live. You don't hold back, even when you want to; you push yourself to keep going. Courage allows you to breathe in the fear and exhale out love for life. You are here for a brief period of time—live it boldly.

Trust in Action

Before you start your day, sit quietly, and give yourself at least fifteen to thirty minutes to listen to music that uplifts and encourages you. Do this before reading your texts, listening to your voice mail, or answering your emails. I recommend listening to instrumental, wordless, upbeat music that allows inspiration to seep in.

As you meditate on the accomplishments you want to achieve, explore and step out of your comfort zone; list your intentions, be specific and detail each goal; timeline your tasks and start your anticipated day.

As you practice this routine each morning, have certainty that, through unwavering faith, you will have the courage to accomplish your goals and dreams. This will set you on your way to achieving day-to-day aspirations and designing your life.

Visual Belief

Visualize yourself accomplishing something that you want to achieve, especially something you never thought you could do. Write down the way you want it to happen, in as much detail as you can. See the end result and do your best not to give up until you achieve it. Understand that you're following a different path than other people, and it's not going to be a straightforward journey.

Be aware of negative self-talk. If you decide, "I can't do this. I don't know how. It's too hard. I don't have the resources. I don't have the money," I can guarantee that you will struggle to achieve what you want. Have the courage to say, "I don't care how long it takes, I'm not giving up."

Watch out for the artificial deadlines that we all impose on ourselves. We use these to trick ourselves into believing we can't accomplish something, so that we can more easily justify giving up. Give yourself a timeline buffer on your goals then set a deadline when you are reaching the finish line. The only right timing is your timing. If God hasn't taken away your burning desire to reach a goal, it's because you are meant to do it. Instead, acknowledge that maybe you aren't ready at the moment, but you will be someday. Then keep moving toward that goal. Go through this process, go through the fear. Walk through it, run through it, whatever you need to do. But do not give up. And visualize yourself there in victory—fulfilled.

Recognize

Do you find yourself living in a constant state of self-doubt? Does indecision hold you back from speaking your deepest truths? Is uncertainty keeping you from going for your boldest dreams and sharing your unique gifts with the world?

It takes a consistent practice of everyday courage to open yourself to new possibilities and transformation. It takes guts to gaze into the future to see where your life may take you. Tap into yourself and understand the gifts that God has bestowed on you. Do not fear this path that is guiding you. It is calling to you for a reason. Surrender to it with passion and determination.

Understand that you are doing this for you and that others will benefit from your bravery. Give your dreams a chance to come alive. Love yourself and know that self-love is going to get you through it all. You deserve this. Commit with passion, purpose, and courage.

True Story of Unwavering Faith

Courage comes from the word "cor," which means "heart" in Latin. The original meaning of courage was to speak from the heart. That is true, for it takes heart to stand up for yourself and protect what is sacred and precious to you. The combination of vulnerability and bravery that lets you open your soul to another person is priceless.

As a young girl, my mother used to send me and my sister to Puerto Rico every summer to visit my great-grandparents. They shared an extraordinary bond, a bond of authentic love. Seeing the way that they cared for each other warmed my heart and spoke to my soul. They were two lovebirds, courting each other as if they had just met a few weeks before. They were young at heart. They lived humble lives and possessed very little, but the love they had for each other gave them everything they needed. They ate, slept, and breathed love, and they shared it in abundance. I knew from an early age that I wanted that kind of devoted relationship that was genuine and everlasting.

In my early teens, my great-grandmother's health began to decline rapidly. Soon, she was diagnosed as terminally ill with only a few weeks to live. My great-grandfather refused financial assistance and prayed to God that my great-grandmother would receive what she needed in her final days—a meaningful and beautiful burial. What he wasn't able to offer monetarily, he made up for this with a lifetime of dedication and genuine love that surpassed any relationship that I ever witnessed as a child.

The story concludes with a financial miracle—he won a local lottery a couple of weeks or so before my great-grandmother passed away, and he received even more money than he needed to pay for the wake and burial. After she passed, my great-grandfather sent the rest of the money to his family in New York. His personal note to us was beautiful. *"This money was a gift from God and the rest, I share with my family."*

My great-grandparents showed me the act of true love is a daily choice—a leap of faith to love someone deeply, wholeheartedly and courageously. I believe in the kind of storybook love that I witnessed between them and choose not to settle for anything less than what is best for me.

Everything we go through in life is to prepare us for what we are meant to become. It manifests into reality when we're ready. If God isn't opening a door right now, it's because it isn't the right door. He has another plan that He will reveal when it's the right season. Have the courage to remain unwaveringly faithful and live life with trust and allowance.

Peace I leave with you; my peace I give you. I do not give to you as the world gives. Do not let your hearts be troubled and do not be afraid.
—John 14:27, NIV

Songs for Courage

Begin your journey to courage with bravery, boldness, and fearless statements. Here is a powerful song of faith, along with an instrumental selection and two secular hits to help you focus as you journal:

- o *Song of faith*
  - – "Miracles" by Colton Dixon
- o *Instrumental music*
  - – "The Power of Will" by Ivan Torrent
- o *Secular songs*
  - – "Brave" by Sara Bareilles
  - – "It's My Life" by Bon Jovi

Journaling for Courage

I believe and receive Courage with Unwavering Faith and envision my life today as:

_____

_____

_____

_____

_____

_____

Jeannie Burgos

Fearlessness is not being without fear. It's doing what you fear in spite of it. To have courage is not only about heroes and heroism. It's also about moral courage (standing up and acting when injustice occurs); intellectual courage (challenging old assumptions and acting to make changes based on new understandings); disciplined courage (remaining steadfast, strategic, and deliberate in the face of inevitable setbacks); and empathic courage (acknowledging personal biases and intentionally moving away from them in order to vicariously experience the trials and triumphs of others). May we practice courage in all its forms so we may become unstoppable.

A life of boldness and confidence disrupts
mediocrity and confinement—choose valor.
—Jeannie Burgos

Poem for Courage

It takes courage to open yourself up to love,
To give of yourself fully and know you are always enough.
Take a chance at life, for mere existence is empty and bland.
Believe in your power and rejoice in God's loving hand.

When you've been defeated, heartbroken, and alone, keep courage near.
Daringly march forward through the fire of fear.
Give your worries to God and drink from His cup.
You will accomplish what you desire if you don't give up.

Dream bigger, better, wiser, and see the world in a different light.
You're stronger, move forward, and know your goals are worth the fight.
Tap into the magic of courage and awaken to possibility.
Love, career, money is within your grasp if you continue to believe.

Photo by Jeannie Burgos

CHAPTER 7

July: Full Abundance

Now to him who is able to do immeasurably
more than all we ask or imagine, according
to his power that is at work within us.
—Ephesians 3:20, NIV

For the Month of July

Get ready to take a leap of faith this month. Trust that financial abundance is headed your way. Do not be consumed about the details of your life and don't try to push or force anything. Instead, maintain your silent confidence, and trust that your faith will set your desire in motion.

Be sure to honor the rewards that have already come to you through your own hard work. Encourage and concentrate on what you desire to bring forth. Let go of the old belief of lack and not enough and embody what is already yours. Let no one nor any circumstance dictate the direction of your journey toward what God has prepared in your name. If He has put it in your heart for good, then run with it, and abundance will cover you.

Be joyful in prayer. Do not come to God in a state of pleading, but ask Him with humble confidence; know that whatever you pray for is already here. A grateful heart opens the door and delivers God's answers. Pray with assuredness and contemplate in the now, as if what you desire has already manifested. You will realize a newfound awareness and strength for mind, body, and soul.

To Achieve Full Abundance through Unwavering Faith

Full abundance is possible. If you are able to dream it, you will be able to embody it, so don't give up. Think about what you have manifested in the past. What have you brought forth with your actions? And how did you bring it forth? Channel your focus and affirm your dreams with distinct certainty. Embrace your desire on a daily basis. Nurture an attitude of gratitude, and God and the universe will provide.

Commit to a daily faith-based practice of abundance and dedication to gratitude. As you start your day with a thankful heart, keep moving forward on your life's journey and notice each blessing as it arises. When you recognize that full abundance is all around you, God will open doors and move mountains that only He can.

There will always be naysayers—people who neither trust nor believe and refuse to recognize God's hand in all that we receive. However, do not allow anyone to take your dream or desire away. Protect yourself from toxic people and allow positive creativity to allocate your time.

Fill your heart with goodness. As you send love to people from that place of abundant overflow, it will come back to you tenfold. Be selfless, and God will always make sure that you will receive in abundance.

Thought

Whatsoever you think about, you will absolutely create, whether it be positive or negative. So, be alert about your feelings and your mindset. If you joyfully pray in gracious gratitude, trusting in divine manifestation, God will make it so in its due time. Focus on the good so that good may result. Recall times when you have attracted opportunities in your life; even if you didn't recognize it at the time, you manifested those good things because you were in a state of gratitude and joy. Now imagine how much power you have when you are intentional about what you want.

God put that burning desire in you so that you would have the drive to follow your dreams. Believe in yourself and trust that He wants you to achieve your goals. No one else can do this for you. People will be there to help you along the way, but never delegate your accomplishments to others. The gift of your achievements will come through you and not through someone else doing them for you.

Trust in God. Trust that He has you in His hands. Even when the path is winding, which it often is, trust that you will get there. The power is in you. And with God's grace, He will make it better than you could ever imagine.

Truth in Wisdom

What I have experienced to be true is that we each uniquely manifest our own abundance. Whether we are aware of it or not, abundance is happening all around us, so why not make it magnificent? Open your heart in discovery of you. Trust in God and don't give up on yourself. Be bold and dream big—make your blessings count and be a godsend to others.

Full abundance is an experience of independence; it's not just monetary freedom but also spiritual openness. Believe that God has brought you to this moment so that what shines within you will be seen without. We all uniquely manifest whatever we think. Trust that when you commit to thinking yourself into full abundance, God will ensure that you receive it in your life.

There will be challenges along the way, but always look for the lesson in the challenge. See the beauty in each challenge; see the gift and the protection. If you understand that life is a rhythm of the seasons, when chaos and distractions appear, they will not influence your drive. You may need to pause, but don't give up.

We all cry sometimes. We feel small and ask God why. Why me? Why this? Have your moment to grieve, mourn, and sulk, but then wipe away your tears and release that tension to God. Ask Him to show you the lesson, the favorable intent of the difficulty. His plans for you are to prosper, not to come to harm; He plans to give you a hope and a future (Jeremiah 29:11). If you embody this verse, you will see His hand in all that you do.

Trust in Action

Money should be used as the instrument that it is. It is currency to exchange. It is a way to offer joy, security, stability, support, and happiness. If you hold onto money tightly and are afraid of losing it, it will leak quickly, like water escaping a strong grip. When you acknowledge that generosity and openhandedness bring abundance, you will manifest it readily.

Choose to help people in hardship instead of fearing that money will run out. You will discover that money is energy, and when you give it away for good purposes, more will come back to you. Don't hold it as a possession; instead, realize that it's a resource. It's a way to communicate in joy and gratitude with others.

Even if you don't have much money, find ways to give. If you see someone in need, find a way to pay for the person's coffee or lunch. Give a cheerful offering to a charity in an amount that you can afford. God multiplies in abundance and delivers value to the heart. Generosity benefits your inner self—body, mind, and spirit.

Visual Belief

Visualize giving to others. Imagine being able to make a difference in the lives of each of your loved ones without any expectation of return. Imagine yourself offering something of great value to each individual and see the look of joy on each of their faces when you do. In your visualization, write them a check to pay off their mortgage, pay off their college debt, book them on a cruise to their dream vacation, help them start a business, give them the keys to a new car, give a substantial donation to a charity that touches their heart. Visualize yourself in full abundance with the ability to share your blessings with the people you love and admire.

Even though this may seem over the top, you want to envision yourself having that kind of money, that kind of currency. Open yourself to the possibility of receiving so much abundance from God that you can joyfully pass it along to your loved ones. May your cup runneth over and over and over.

Visualize more than you can ever conceive and believe that God has you and will bring it forth. Envision without delay and keep it close to your heart. The magnificence of full abundance through unwavering faith may open doors to fruitful riches you've only dreamed of.

Recognize

Recognize that, if you ask in good spirit for full abundance to come to others, it will boomerang and come back to you. Abundance is here and now. All you have to do is have faith with benevolence.

Don't ever quit on your dreams. They are waiting on you. If your dreams are for good, God will guide you through and make it a reality. Wayne Dyer once said, "Doing what you love is the cornerstone of having abundance in your life." Follow your passion and live with expectancy that good will come from it.

Recognize the miracles that happen in other people's lives. Delight in their achievements and accomplishments. Why? Because they never gave up. They recognized it was for them. When you practice unwavering faith in full abundance, God sees your heart and your intent. He sees that your desire for wealth is to share and not to hoard. He will bless you and give you what you ask in multitude.

True Story of Unwavering Faith

I woke up one November morning in 2019 thinking it was going to be an ordinary day. To my surprise and dismay, it was raining in my garage. The dishwasher was programmed to wash the night before and malfunctioned overnight and damaged the entire space. I was shaken, yet I had to collect myself and pray for God's guidance to get through it. I prayed that He would bring forth the best outcome to this calamity. I knew I had to release my tension and give it to God. Momentarily, after wiping the tears away, I felt calm and reassured it would all turn out better than I could envision. Being in the state of gratitude gave me the peace of mind that I so needed.

I was grateful for each person that helped me through this ordeal—from my understanding boss to the customer service at my insurance company to the repairmen and cleaning company. The repairmen put me at ease; they assured me that they would fix my garage and make it even better than before. Surrendering my worries to God opened doors to full abundance, and it showed up without delay.

As the workmen were getting close to leaving that first day, I heard God's whisper, *"Ask them to move the dishwasher; ask them to move the dishwasher."*

It wasn't their job, but I asked them to please move the dishwasher to measure it for a new one. One of the workers noticed a serious issue. He called me over and said, *"This leak was a blessing in disguise. The wires were burning. They were so hot they melted the caps off. If this leak didn't happen, you would have had an electrical fire."*

I was stunned by this news, but my shock quickly gave way to gratitude. From this water damage, God saved my home and possibly my life and my daughters' lives. I told myself not to worry about the work or to rush it; I was cheerful and appreciative throughout, because I knew what could have been the alternative.

The blessing and lesson about the incident is that, months before the damage, I was praying for the opportunity to redecorate my garage into a family room. I wanted to have space to exercise, room for my car, and a comfortable place to have fun with family and friends. The destruction was a miracle in disguise. Through it, God protected and gave us more than we expected.

Ask for full and plenty with unwavering faith, and God will provide it to you in ways that are greater than you can even imagine.

And God is able to bless you abundantly, so that in all things at all times, having all that you need, you will abound in every good work.
—2 Corinthians 9:8, NIV

Songs for Full Abundance

Begin your journey to full abundance with motivation, confidence, and forward-looking statements. Here is a powerful song of faith, along with an instrumental selection and two secular hits to help you focus as you journal:

- o *Song*
  - – "Higher" by For All Seasons
- o *Instrumental music*
  - – "Hero Memories" by Epic Soul Factory
- o *Secular songs*
  - – "When You Believe" by Whitney Houston & Mariah Carey
  - – "Diamonds" by Rihanna

Journaling for Full Abundance

I believe and receive full abundance with unwavering faith and envision my life today as:

_____

_____

_____

_____

_____

_____

Jeannie Burgos

Know with absolute certainty that full abundance is in you. You already have the power within to achieve anything you are inspired to accomplish. Allow the power to flow and understand that it may take time to reach your goals; however, keep your faith that what you desire is here and now. Commit to living your dreams and stop making excuses. The time is now.

> *A grateful heart opens the door to full abundance. Once*
> *you discover it, influence and inspire others to believe.*
> —Jeannie Burgos

Poem for Full Abundance

Full abundance is to be grateful for what you already own
To allow God's grace to provide in assortment and overflow.
It is giving to others in both hardship and modest need
So you may always attract your heart's desire and graciously receive.

Full abundance offers love, riches, generosity, and happiness.
It is God's way of gifting us with His benevolent kindness.
It offers optimism, hope, and brightness from life's challenges
So we may be mindful and offer a hand with delightfulness.

May unwavering faith guide the fearful, anxious, and lost
To grow and flourish in wisdom and undisputed trust.
May we always remain grateful and genuinely humble,
For God will carry us when we inevitably stumble.

Photo by Jeannie Burgos

CHAPTER 8

August: Passion

And we know that for those who love God all
things work together for good, for those who
are called according to His purpose.
—Romans 8:28; NIV

For the Month of August

Push yourself toward your unspoken passion. Assist and give service through the use of your natural gifts, interests, and the things you are passionate about.

Do what you love, and the money will follow. Give recognition and a voice to your knowledge and inquisitiveness. You will help others who are searching for what you have to offer. Travel, spend time with yourself, do new things, meditate, introspect and do not lose faith.

Your hunger needs to be fed; offer it something extraordinary.

To Achieve Passion through Unwavering Faith

Feel what a gift it is to be alive. God chose you and the spirit and essence that is within you for a purpose. When you bring forth the passion that lives within you, you will open yourself up to discovering why you are here and what you are meant to do in your life.

Do not allow the old story of why your life hasn't gone the way that you wanted keep you from manifesting what is yours. The accounts may vary from unsupportive family members to bullies to heartbreaks to ageism to forgotten dreams. Whatever the story is, your old mindset will only keep you reliving the past and not discovering the new. You can't undo the past; what has happened has happened, and it has also made you who you are.

The challenges you have experienced along the way have been opportunities to grow and get to know yourself during periods of adversity. Open your eyes to the realization that God breathed you into being so that you could learn to live with passion. God wants you to realize the gifts that He has given you so that you can contribute and be witness to the beauty of the life that surrounds you.

Allow God's sweet whisper to guide your every step and open the door to your best life yet. Life will bring conflicts and struggles. Through those challenges, you will learn valuable lessons and grow closer to your greatness. When you truly take the time to look at the gift that you are, you will find the strength to bring forth the passion that is within you.

Thought

Ignite your passion—believe that you will achieve your heartfelt desire. Unwavering faith changes everything within you no matter the circumstances around you. Even if you don't know anyone else in your life who has achieved the things that you want to accomplish, understand that your dreams will still manifest for you. Make your dreams vivid, tangible in the present tense, and breathe them to life. See yourself as where you need to be in order to ignite your passion and discover your purpose.

Pray for guidance, and listen—be alert for answers. Have faith in what you are seeking, and trust that God will provide for you when the time is right. Be excited about the things that drive your passion. Elevate your state to compel the manifestation of what you desire. See what you wish for as already in your grasp. Envision yourself smiling and laughing, surrounded by those who love and support you, as you celebrate achieving what you have manifested.

If you have a dream of owning a floral boutique, opening a dance studio, writing a book, running a marathon, or traveling the world—visualize your goal as distinctive as possible. Design how you desire to experience it. For instance, see yourself opening the door in the morning to your beautiful floral boutique, breathe in the gentle smell of the flowers and scented candles, see the gorgeous display of orchids and roses, and hear the consistent ring of door chimes and the many dedicated clients coming in to buy your floral designs. Feel how fulfilling it is to be where you have dreamed of being. Believe with unwavering faith that you will make it, and one day you just may.

Practice this kind of visualized belief. Believe passionately, and trust that it will be so. Don't go back to doubting just because it hasn't happened yet. Keep seeing yourself doing what you love and recognize that this is something that you are meant to achieve. Know that God wants you to become the best version of yourself. When you commit to your dreams, He will walk with you.

Truth in Wisdom

What I have experienced to be true is that passionate commitment to our dreams bring us closer to achieving them. It's in God's timing; you will reach your goal. Don't be discouraged if you need to take a detour. This is God's way of teaching you new life lessons along your path, and ultimately achieve them.

I adhere to God's whisper. I trust that He is guiding me and protecting me. I have seen God manifest what I want in my life when I surrender and allow Him to lead me to it. Ask, allow, follow and find your passion and believe that God will create the path for you to get there. It takes action, but He makes the way.

So often, we try to control what God is manifesting for us. We think we know best, we put ourselves in the middle, and we struggle against God's current. There is a Chinese proverb that says, "Don't push the river; it flows by itself." The river will move as it is meant to. Don't fight the current; respect it.

Be open. Make the commitment to follow the current and finish what you want to accomplish. So long as it is something that brings you joy, keep going with the flow, and you will achieve it. Passion through unwavering faith sustains your motivation. It keeps you feeling alive, and it brings out the warrior that is within you.

Trust in Action

Each week this month, write down a short list of five or six things that spark your passion and excite and accelerate your senses. This doesn't have to be a daily practice; however, find time a few days each week and give yourself at least thirty to sixty minutes. I find that it helps to play inspirational music while you do this to keep yourself in a creative and productive frame of mind. Write down each passion, no matter how outrageous it might seem. Your list can contain things you have always wanted to do, as well as things you love and want to do more. Each day you write your list, there will be some items that repeat from previous lists and some items that pop up new. The items that keep showing up are persistent passions that God is bringing to you for a reason. If you take notice of the repetitive calling, that is an indication that you should pursue it.

Throughout the week, look for opportunities to incorporate these passions into your life in a way that is meaningful and also achievable. If volunteering keeps showing up on your list, look for opportunities to volunteer within your community. Even if you don't pursue it as a career, it can be a fulfilling interest. Your passion can also tell you other things about yourself. For some people, a passion for flowers could be a sign to move from a cold climate to a place where flowers bloom all year round.

Listen to your passions and find ways to bring them into your life. Your passions help you combat the mundane routine of existing day after day and give you the opportunity to live vibrantly. Pay attention to your heart and where it is guiding you. Write down your passions without judgment or criticism and believe that, if this is something you want to do, God will guide your way to manifest it.

Follow your passions, and perhaps they can lead you to the best part of your life. And why not? We had so much passion when we were children, and most have forgotten what that feels like. Rediscover that child that is still within you and believe in miracles again!

Visual Belief

Passion is not just existing; it's living. Passion is understanding that we have one life—it is the only life we are going to remember. Find the gratitude in living so you can make this life as special as possible. Be passionate about what you can learn from the challenges and hardships in your life. Be passionate about finding the love and happiness you deserve. Be passionate about understanding certain things you need to let go of and certain things you need to allow.

Close your eyes, and as you breathe, take your time and feel the appreciation for the moment. Breathe in what you want to bring into being. Give thanks for what God is going to manifest for you. Practice breathing exercises before you do a task that you're passionate about. Thank God for what He is going to make real for you. He will bring forth what is in you, and you will be able to express it in the way it is supposed to come through.

Practice gratitude as you breathe your passion into reality. Allow yourself to let go of your present concerns every time you breathe out. Use your breathing to elevate your state and tap into a place of passion. It is effective to listen to fearless inspirational music when you do this. Listening to music is one of the quickest ways to change your state. Once you feel yourself in a place of mindful focus, this is a good time to write your list of passions for the day.

Breathe in what you want to see. Breathe it in, and there it is... Once you can see it in your mind, you know you can manifest it and make it a reality. It's no longer a thing in the distance that may or may not come to pass; instead, it's right here, right now.

Recognize

Passion is true commitment. It is understanding that a decision is yours if you choose it. Passion is up to you to decide how far you want to go with it. No matter what, don't give up. Once you have discovered what your passion is, you are bound to succeed, because you will give it your all.

Passion is contagious. It allows you to help others reach their goals. Deep down, we are all here to help each other; we are all here to serve. You will experience the greatest fulfilment when you are able to change someone else's life for good from a place of love.

If you cut yourself off from passion, you may flow along, but you won't have the same spark that makes you commit to what you're doing. Passion leads to success—and not just financial success. Money is important; however, the goal should always be joy, and passion is joyful commitment. Passion is a promise to lead your best life. Why not start that today?

True Story of Unwavering Faith

One day, I decided that, no matter what, I am going to follow my passion, which is to be an inspirational best-selling author. My passion is to keep writing after my first book is published. For a long time, fear held me prisoner and kept me from starting this book. My passionate commitment to my dream pulled me through that fear and allowed me to keep going. It is my ultimate goal to use my words to encourage others along their own journeys of unwavering faith.

I had my garage destroyed by a colossal water damage right in the middle of finishing this book. I asked God, What is the lesson that I need to learn here? I didn't want this to be yet another excuse to delay completing my book. My lesson has been to keep going and follow my passion, no matter what adversity might arise to block the way. I no longer see the things that befall me as a deterrent; instead, they have inspired me to make my writing a priority. My passion for writing has opened my world and has reinforced my faith in God's whisper. Faith is something I believe with my entire soul, and I now have a faithful pursuit of what I want to achieve.

Obstacles will arise and change the timing of your goal. Scripture tells us, "Keep on asking, and you will receive what you ask for. Keep on seeking, and you will find. Keep on knocking, and it will be opened to you" (Matthew 7:7, NLT). When you finally commit to doing something with passion, it turns from a *should* into a *must*. Something that is a must is integral to your core. You no longer say to yourself, "I really should do this," or "I really need to do that." Instead you say, "I must do this, and so I will."

Truly, truly, I say to you, whoever believes in me will also
do the works that I do; and greater works than these
will he do, because I am going to the Father.
—John 14:12, ESV

Songs for Passion

Begin your journey to passion with drive, confidence, and purposeful statements. Here is a powerful song of faith, along with an instrumental selection and two secular hits to help you focus as you journal:

- *Song of faith*
  - "Confidence" by Sanctus Real
- *Instrumental music*
  - "A New Dawn, A New Beginning" by Fearless Motivation Instrumentals (Epic Music)
- *Secular songs*
  - "One in a Million" by Ne-Yo
  - "Love on Top" by Beyoncé

Journaling for Passion

I believe and receive passion with unwavering faith and envision my life today as:

_____

_____

_____

_____

_____

Jeannie Burgos

Your passions will fill your empty cup until it is brimming with the experiences and opportunities that you have always wanted in life. Don't be afraid. Follow what you love to do. Write down your passions, envision yourself doing them, and you will see how God will open doors and lead you to a better place than you could ever imagine. Have a present-tense experience in all of your senses of what you want to manifest in your life. Devote yourself to making it happen. Ignite your passion for life so that it is no longer conceptual but tangible and something that you can move toward.

Decide to embrace the gift of life and release your passion!
—Jeannie Burgos

Poem for Passion

To live with passion is the driving force to success;
You breathe in desire and exhale indifference.
Passion is a hunger—an appetite for abundance.
We gain strength, make vivid decisions, and move with significance.

Passion transforms our lives from existing to being.
It allows us to excel, take chances, and value our feelings.
Passion is an intense emotion, the excitement we have for our desires;
It kindles our love, our dreams, and fuels us with an eternal fire.

Live with passion! It motivates and grants us reasons to climb.
The invisible ladder of desire, it urges us onward to attain the prize
Called life—live it courageously, unwaveringly, and with an open mind.
Decide with all your heart, commit, and cherish each moment in time.

Photo by Jeannie Burgos

CHAPTER 9

September: Joy

May the God of hope fill you with all joy and
peace in believing, so that by the power of the
Holy Spirit you may abound in hope.
—Romans 15:13, ESV

For the Month of September

This month, practice living your days full of joy. Joy is a powerful, sustaining feeling of gratitude and love. Joy is different than happiness, which is a fleeting emotion that ranges from contentment and satisfaction to bliss and intense pleasure. Happiness is based on outward circumstances, material objects, and temporary feelings.

Joy, however, is a choice purposefully made. It is of the spirit infused with comfort and peace. Joy is a practice and a behavior—deliberate and intentional. It's the heart and of the soul. Joy endures hardship and trials and connects with meaning and purpose. A person pursues happiness but chooses joy. It is the experience when you see your child, who is your pride and joy.

Joy is a pure, deep feeling that surfaces from within and connects you to God. Joy keeps your heart gentle and beating for others. It makes you aware to love and to accept and place judgment aside.

To Achieve Joy through Unwavering Faith

Take time to reflect and find what brings joy in your life. Open yourself up to spiritual experiences; look for ways to care for others; go deep within yourself to find profound gratitude; seek inward peace and bask in thankfulness. This will start the process of opening your heart and feeling appreciation for the essence of life around you.

Take time to serve others selflessly and quietly. Assist others in a way that brings you joy through the act of giving without expectation of reward, or outside praise for your generosity. Being of service is something that will bring you joy every day.

This exemplifies the difference between happiness and joy. When people say they want to feel happy, they are describing an emotion that is fleeting, just like sadness or anger. Happiness comes and goes, yet joy remains. It is deeply felt and continual, even through adversity and unfortunate circumstances.

You can simultaneously feel sadness and joy. An example is when a loved one passes; you can feel profound sorrow and also great joy that you were able to spend time with this person during their life and create so many memorable memories with them.

Many people think they should be happy all the time, but it's unreasonable to think that we're going to experience constant happiness. Your emotions come and go, flowing naturally. There will be days when you aren't happy at all, but you can remain joyful through unwavering faith and consider, this too shall pass.

Thought

When you think of joy, picture a sudden burst of gratitude that resounds in your soul and captures your heart. It's an inner glow that manifests as your aura—a shine that emanates from within you. When you start to experience joy in your life, other people will see it as a twinkle in your eyes, a magnetic smile, pleasant to be around. As they say, your eyes are the windows to your soul—be the light.

Envision yourself in a state of harmonious serenity. See yourself offering joy to others. Bring encouragement and hope to those around you.

Wicked things do happen every day—wars, economic collapse, natural disasters, and pandemics will befall us. It's important to be aware of current events and do what we can to aid those who have been affected by these tragedies; however, we will not be successful at helping others if we are crippled by despair.

When you express joy to others, you help them see that there is hope and a path forward. It is a simple way to inspire. As you pray and meditate, see yourself connected to others so that you can make a difference with a good and kind heart.

Truth in Wisdom

What I have experienced to be true is that when I feel great joy; it's because I am connected to God and adhere to His word. It's a feeling of elation and a personal relationship with the divine that has increased over the course of my life. It has taken me many years to get to where I am now. Even when I was far from Him and thought I could do it all myself, He was still there with me. When I am connected to God and take time to be grateful for everything I have, I feel His presence that elates my state and keeps me in the moment.

I find joy in connecting with young children and witnessing their blissful innocence, inquisitiveness, and thirst for learning. Giving selflessly brings me joy. I experience joy when I step beyond the transient sensation of happiness and take in the gratitude I feel for life. Joy can be accessed at any time by changing your disposition and filling yourself with confidence, faith, passion, and love. Joy is your birthright—claim it!

Trust in Action

Joy is something to tap into every day. Make joy a daily practice. This month, take thirty minutes each day, whether it is in the morning, afternoon, or evening. Take time for yourself and seek out inspirational stories that bring life to your soul.

There is a barrage of negative exchange that is hurled at us day in and day out. Positive comments are not as pervasive as negative comments, which are widespread like wildfire. Keep away as much as possible from the constant pessimism that others express. You can always find information about bad things that are happening in the world—we are inundated by it—so purposefully look for things that are joyful.

Find articles, books, videos, and podcasts that inspire you. Realize that you are part of something bigger. Seek out people who have gone through great struggles and triumphed. Listen to encouraging and stimulating music. Music can change your mood in an instant and take you to a place where joy flows freely. Take time to discover what joy looks like for you—come out of your shell and explore.

Have the unwavering faith that life is joyful and that you have the ability to bring cheer to others. When you choose joy, you become the light of change and positively influence someone else's life. Ask God to give you the eyes to see the good in everything.

Call joy from your heart. We receive what we ask for (deliberately or involuntarily). Some may see misfortune as their predominate thought and that's what materializes. But if you're seeking the good, great and exceptional, you will be witness to God's favor in your life and others. Before you know it, you'll realize that it's effortless to choose joy. Take time for yourself—laugh, surround yourself with optimistic people, and give yourself permission to be in a blissful state.

Visual Belief

Imagine something you have desired for years coming true. Imagine your loved ones succeeding in their careers. Imagine the one you've prayed for finally coming into your life like a dream come true. Imagine the joy of having children or adopting a child into your family. Imagine the purchase of your first home or another occasion that is equally as important.

Bask in the excitement that you feel when you visualize these miracles happening. Really see yourself there and believe you are living it. Picture yourself where you want to be, not where you are. Allow the brightness of joy to illuminate where you want to go.

Little by little, as you continue this exercise every day, you will start moving in the direction of these things that you desire. Your goals will be dreams fulfilled in real time. You will experience more and more joy each time you visualize them coming to fruition. Open your heart and your soul and know that joy can be yours whenever you choose it.

Recognize

God is with us every step of the way. Through hardships, we can rebuild even better than before. Always do your best to find the good in what happens. It's important to maintain a hopeful outlook.

Don't allow negative occurrences to suppress you; they arise to offer you the opportunity to grow wiser—not to fear. God has a bigger plan— there are reasons why incidents happen the way they do. Pray for the eyes to see, the ears to listen and the heart to empathize and you will emanate joy—believe it!

True Story of Unwavering Faith

As a single parent, I have experienced the complexities of motherhood. I have taken on more than I should and have had to push through the struggles with very little help. However, my two daughters have added joy to my life and given me so much wisdom, inspiration, determination, blessings and love throughout the years.

Before I became a mother, I sought happiness but it was fleeting, unsustainable, short-lived. I searched for happiness through love, yet I was fearful of losing it. I stayed in relationships longer than I should have—only to lose myself in it. But when I became a mother, I lived enthused through their smiles and loving hugs. I knew that happiness is fleeting and joy is purposefully made. To witness my daughters rise with good hearts from a divorced home brings me tears of bliss.

Joy is to be realized every day. Take the time to decompress, slow down, rest, and relax when your body and mind needs it. You will be able to focus better, take in the moment and choose ease instead of worry. Then bask in joy for the small and great things in your life. With unwavering faith, you can experience the enduring power of joy.

> *Consider it pure joy, my brothers and sisters, whenever*
> *you face trials of many kinds because you know that*
> *the testing of your faith produces perseverance.*
> —James 1:2–3, NIV

Songs for Joy

Begin your journey to joy with gladness, gratitude, and purposeful statements. Here is a powerful song of faith, along with an instrumental selection and two secular hits to help you focus as you journal:

- o *Song of faith*
  - – "Joy" by King & Country
- o *Instrumental music*
  - – ""Spirit of the Wild" by BrunuhVille
- o *Secular songs*
  - – "Can't Stop the Feeling" by Justin Timberlake
  - – "Girl on Fire" by Alicia Keys

Journaling for Joy

I believe and receive joy with unwavering faith and envision my life today as:

_____

_____

_____

_____

_____

_____

_____

_____

_____

_____

_____

_____

_____

_____

_____

_____

_____

_____

_____

_____

_____

Joy is in the spirit. It is love, peace, patience, kindness, and faithfulness. Joy is something you feel from your soul. It is the pure elation when you see your little one walk for the first time. Joy conveys virtue. It is the love and goodness that you bring to all those you touch. What a gift it is to offer joy and let people see that it is in them, too. God gave you the ability to share joy. It is a gift to demonstrate. No matter who you are, you have that capacity within you. Joy will get you through anything in life. No matter how dark things become, if you have joy, you will be able to rebuild and be in an even better state than you were before.

> *If you live your entire life on a strict diet, how*
> *will you ever taste the flavor of joy?*
> -Jeannie Burgos

Poem for Joy

Joy is a treasure to offer and keep.
It's an inner peace—sacred and sweet.
It is timeless and pure and tenderly deep.
It's no fleeting emotion but a blissful, steady beat.

When we live in joy, it is wonder, gratitude, delight, and pleasure.
It offers awareness when we are in sorrow, grief, and at odds with each other.
Joy is an understanding—a knowing—a lasting satisfaction;
It's the guiding light to our hearts and the driving force to motivation.

How magnificent the gentle guide, the glow vibrating with pure elation.
To live in joy, we must let go of regrets, worry, and desolation.
We have one life; to make the best of it with appreciation,
Joy will bring the promise of youth, love, wonder, and celebration.

Photo by Jeannie Burgos

CHAPTER 10

October: Wisdom

Blessed are those who find wisdom,
those who gain understanding
—Proverbs 3:13, NIV

For the Month of October

Gain wisdom this month; try new things; talk to new people from different cultures and backgrounds; be open to unlike perspectives and outcomes. Wisdom cannot be taught; however, knowledge becomes wisdom. Knowledge speaks—wisdom listens. Wisdom is a deep understanding; it is refined by experience, which helps us develop the skills to support it. We gain wisdom through discretion and maturity.

Take the time for a good read, seek out wise mentors, choose to learn what you love and intensely comprehend. Wisdom evokes the rich attributes of insight, clear judgment, and nonattachment. These enduring virtues will carry you sagely through life. When challenges and struggle arise, seek inner guidance, as well as learning from those who have already been through the trenches. Trying new things and reflecting on the process gives you the ability to gain wisdom; however, don't always take the long and hard road when you can learn from your elders and others who have evolved from their hardest times. There is wisdom in seeking knowledge from those who have experienced life's difficulties so you can avoid the same pitfalls. When you learn, you grow; appreciate your progress and share your wisdom.

To achieve Wisdom through Unwavering Faith

We obtain wisdom in many forms. We acquire wisdom through pain, which is the hardest way and often the most life altering. We also experience wisdom through achievement and reward, as we learn the processes that work for success. We achieve wisdom through contemplation, reflecting on the experiences of life to see what they may teach us. We gain wisdom by learning the active ingredients of other people's triumphs and taking the shortcuts that their life stories teach us. We attain wisdom by being inquisitive, asking questions, and discerning.

Wisdom can be achieved through many different means. Explore, expand, be flexible. You have countless people to learn from, and many have made their stories available to you through books, podcasts, seminars, and other forms of media. You don't have to reinvent the wheel yourself each time you wish to learn something new. All you have to do is reach out and you will discover that it is within your grasp.

Thought

Be intentional and learn from those who have become successful in ways that you admire. Reverse engineer the steps they took to arrive at their accomplishments. Focus on areas that are of high interest to you so that you may follow through and prosper. Whenever you put your attention toward something that you consider important, you will be more likely to do your best. You will strive to succeed as you enjoy the process.

Find motivation in following a proven path. Learn as much as you can about the leaders you esteem. Discover the active ingredients of their success and create a recipe that works for you.

This is the process that Napoleon Hill used in his groundbreaking Depression-era book, *Think and Grow Rich*. Instead of relying on repeated failure to define his life lessons, he analyzed the lives of numerous leaders in business and industry and developed success strategies based on their career paths. Pain is unfortunately our most common teacher, but we can still reach for another way.

Truth in Wisdom

What I have experienced to be true is, when I take the time to reflect, contemplate, and pray for guidance on a situation I'm experiencing, God will offer direction through scripture, a loss, an inspirational teaching, a heartbreak, a financial challenge, a promotion, a new relationship, a milestone reached—his ways are limitless. Ask God, *"What must I learn from this experience so I may grow, prosper, bless, and forgive?"* Refrain from blaming, and simply observe the wisdom He brings to you through His whisper.

Learn to be in tune with the chances that show up. From bumping into a friend at the store to finding an inspirational book at the bookshop or online to feeling the sudden urge to call an old colleague. Each of these occurrences may bring you the insight you seek if you are open to receiving it. Be unrestricted and ask the right questions of the universe, and God will answer with insightful sensitivity.

Trust in Action

Take time every weekend this month and write and refine your greater purpose and life mission. Search for the intuitive maturity that lies within you—it is waiting to be activated. Allow growth to come in rapid form for your benefit and to serve others. Read aloud what you have written and trust that you can make your mission possible. If you have asked for God's wisdom, the answer you seek will show up.

Believe, God will show you the purpose and mission that are meant for you. Come to God with intention and unequivocal faith that it will come to pass. His benevolence usually comes as a whisper, not a shout. It is an intuitive embrace. When it shows up, pay attention, and take steps to becoming wiser and more generous of heart in relationships, career, parenthood, and all the other important facets of your life.

Visual Belief

Envision yourself as the director of your own life movie. You get to guide every scene and direct your life according to your screenplay. Remember, your story is bigger than just you. Others will help you tell the movie of your life—so make it box office worthy.

You are the director, producer, writer, and main character. Take the time to wisely lay out what you want to manifest. You are the one telling your story, and you get to create your life as you want it to unfold. Have ownership over who you are, and trust that God will guide you through it.

Recognize

Wisdom is an expression of a deep understanding that resonates with your spirit. Anyone can become knowledgeable about a subject by reading, researching, memorizing facts but wisdom is knowing when to say it. Discernment and humility will be your guide.

Pray for guidance and insight and recognize that He will bring people into your life for you to model. The principle of modeling states that, if one person can achieve something, anyone can learn to do it. Become a soul detective, and you can uncover your path to success. Look for the strategies they used and incorporate some of their life lessons.

Seek out ways to learn that are enjoyable and interesting. Learning that lifts you up and makes you feel good about yourself is much more effective than learning that tears you down and makes you feel inadequate. Recognize that, at any point in your journey, you can begin to change and grow and achieve the success that you want in your life—wise up and rise up.

True Story of Unwavering Faith

I find great wisdom when I exercise various forms of teachings. When I read scripture; spend quality time with elders; listen to successful inspirational leaders and spiritual advisors; physically relax, pray and meditate; I grow. It's a balance approach to life and develops through mastery in defining moments.

Our teachers are important because they show us the paths to take and paths to avoid. The doors to cross and the doors to close. They have learned through pain, regret, and self-reflection how to arrive in life. I have received important lessons from reading the words of those who have come before me. I journal everyday with appreciation and voice the intention out loud. This practice has allowed me to surrender and accept the now and what is to come. Throughout my life, I had the need to please (to a fault). It was difficult to put myself first and I could not say no to those in my life. I sacrificed and yielded more than I should have. However, it wasn't until I made the wise choice to surrender the need to please, that my life took a turn for the better. I surrender my trials to God. I practice releasing the uneasy feeling of saying no until it becomes comfortable. When I say yes, I show up delighted and intentional, because I graciously want to. I have lived enough to know that the key to living sensible is to live in the moment. When you reside with love, empathy, faith, open-mindedness, generosity, forgiveness, and joy, your choices will be in good judgment.

Tip the scales so that your growth comes more from the observation of other people's success than through the personal experience of pain and sorrow. Even if you never hit a true low point in your life, you can still save yourself years of unfocused attempts at progress by learning other people's life lessons. Why waste time with stress and suffering when you don't have to?

> *Teach us to number our days, that we may gain a heart of wisdom.*
> —Psalms 90:12, NIV

Songs for Wisdom

Begin your journey to wisdom with reason, insight, and purposeful statements. Here is a powerful song of faith, along with an instrumental selection and two secular hits to help you focus as you journal:

- o *Song of faith*
  - – "Different" by Micah Tyler
- o *Instrumental music*
  - – "Warrior" by The BionicSkin (inspiration emotional aggressive rap beat)
- o *Secular songs*
  - – "Broken & Beautiful" by Kelly Clarkson
  - – "Just the Way You Are" by Bruno Mars

Journaling for Wisdom

I believe and receive wisdom with unwavering faith and envision my life today as:

_____

_____

_____

_____

_____

Jeannie Burgos

_____

_____

_____

_____

_____

_____

_____

_____

_____

_____

_____

_____

_____

_____

_____

_____

_____

_____

Understand you don't have to hit rock bottom in order to start climbing to where you want to go. Learn from people who went through unimaginable loss and came out triumphant on the other side. You can learn from people who did not have the benefit of generational wealth and built their life with their own two hands. You can learn from the people who have experienced failure so you may steer clear from defeat and follow their lead to a life of success.

> *Stop excusing your life away—I've never met*
> *anyone who came back to do it all over again.*
> —Jeannie Burgos

Poem for Wisdom

Wisdom is a welcome intelligence.
It bears an insightful and delightful gift.
We escape the grips of irrationality
And receive an enlightened lift.

Wisdom is a treasured understanding,
Embracing development, good sense, and thoughtful learning.
We aspire to mature from limiting beliefs
As we create, improve, and naturally receive.

Once we acknowledge the cycle of our desires,
The challenges, the questions, how faith empowers,
We welcome wisdom to the center of our essence
And let go of old identities to adopt a sage, genuine presence.

Photo by Jeannie Burgos

CHAPTER 11

November: Empathy and Compassion

Be completely humble and gentle; be patient,
bearing with one another in love.
—Ephesians 4:2, NIV

For the Month of November

This month, grow through acts of empathy and compassion. You offer a powerful gift to those who need an understanding hand, a shoulder to cry on, or a sympathetic hug. You have the capacity to make all the difference in the world to those who need it.

Empathy is the ability to take the perspective of another person's feelings and emotions and understand what the person is going through in a situation. Compassion is when those feelings and emotions motivate you with the desire to help.

Learn to offer this gift without losing yourself in another's suffering. Set your internal boundaries so that you do not pour from a hollow cup and lose yourself in the process. Be kind, gentle, and patient with yourself and those you seek to comfort.

To Achieve Empathy and Compassion through Unwavering Faith

To become more understanding and tenderhearted, take the time to walk in someone else's shoes. Contemplate what it feels like to endure a loss, a breakup, or a traumatic event. Whatever the other person's situation might be, place your heart there.

You may not know exactly what their hardship feels like; however, we have all experienced a misfortune that may have brought us to our knees. Comprehending another person's sorrow allows you to support them in their time of need. Let them share their heart with you. Most of the time, what the other person needs is a listening ear, an open mind, and words of understanding.

Thought

As you take the time to listen to another person's pain, give them center stage to express their emotions. At the same time, exercise healthy limits. If you transfer their hurt into your core, you will end up breaking your heart in the process. You are more helpful to others when you remain steadfastly supportive and do not allow yourself to be afflicted by the waves of their emotions.

Empathy and compassion are essential skills to practice. They teach us to become emotionally intelligent as we learn how to actively listen to other people's stories of adversity and triumph. Thoughtfulness and concern are divine. The harmonious bonds you form through acts of kindness and care may change the world for someone in need.

Truth in Wisdom

My father passed away two years ago. This experience created a void that is deep and unique to all who have suffered the loss of a parent. Times like this are when you truly need your loved ones to be the soft place to fall; they allow you to grieve with a supportive hand on your shoulder and a box of tissues at the ready. Show compassion by holding a friend's hand, allowing them to cry, listening to their grief, cooking them a hot meal, or sitting with them in quiet understanding. This balance of love, presence, and strength soothes the heartbroken through their time of grief.

Be open with your heart as you listen to their memories; be there with your hands as you aid them at home; be there with your steadfastness as you hold them through their sorrow. Take on what you can, for the support is appreciated more than you could ever know. As Maya Angelou once said, *"I think we all have empathy. We may not have enough courage to display it."* Have the courage—your humble strength reveals the kindness of your heart.

Trust in Action

This month, dedicate time each week to think about people you know who would appreciate a phone call, a visit, or an outing to a movie or a restaurant. Perhaps you know someone who has gone through a divorce and is longing for some kindness and compassion. You may have a friend who is a recent empty nester and having difficulty adjusting to life without children at home. Perhaps someone you know has had a recent health crisis or has been laid off from a job.

Whatever your friends are going through, open your heart to them. Extend a hand and let them know that you care. Reassure them that no matter where they are on their path, you are there to listen and encourage them. Take the steps to connect with them and offer nonjudgmental support and understanding.

Visual Belief

Close your eyes and in your mind's eye, picture someone in your life with whom you have a challenging relationship. Make a commitment to reach out to them in love and light—be the friend you desire to have. As you connect with people you have struggled with, give them your unconditional acceptance and understanding.

While you meditate, envision yourself sitting together with them and try to see things through their eyes. Share how you feel; acknowledge their pain; be encouraging, and show gratitude for their openness. Appreciate that empathy is something that everyone needs. Imagine yourself extending your hands to them and offering them forgiveness and recognition.

Remember, no matter what history you may share, we are all children of God. God forgives them as He forgives you.

Recognize

It requires inner-work to experience the full blessing of compassion. Compassion is an action. It is heartfelt—full of grace and gratitude. At the same time, it's important to distinguish that your ability to express compassion and empathy has a limit, which is based on the energy that you have available to give.

If you allow yourself to be overwhelmed with your empathy for others to the point of being weakened by your emotions, you will do a disservice to yourself and everyone around you. Do not allow empathy to drain your cup dry. Fill your cup to overflow, and you will have an abundance to give.

True Story of Unwavering Faith

From the time I was a young child, I have fostered empathy and compassion, often without realizing it. I have frequently been called the sensitive one— receptive to people's moods, and caring for those in sorrow.

Being vulnerable, compassionate, and considerate is most vital when a loss is experienced. My dear father arrived at his last phase of life in March 2019. My sisters and I had one of our hardest trials ahead of us. Prayer was in the forefront of our hearts as we made the arrangements to travel to Puerto Rico to be by his side. We asked God for a miracle, willing our father to make it at least until we got there.

He was isolated in the hospital and in a grave state. With limited visitation available, my older sister and I were given the opportunity to gather around him and embrace him in the hopes he would awaken from his coma. When we walked into his room, he sensed our presence. Once he heard our voices and prayers, he opened his eyes in acknowledgement! We embraced him and squeezed his hands, praying over him with tears of joy and gratitude that he had waited for us.

The doctors and nurses knew him well in ICU were surprised and elated that he had awoken. They told us, *"He must have been waiting for his children to come."* He had been unresponsive for days. He was intubated, and his heart was very weak. He could not speak, and yet he spoke to us as he responded to our commands to squeeze our hand, open his eyes, and wiggle his toes.

My sisters and I took turns to be with him, comfort him, and pray over him, which gave him peace and rest. We had to return home, but he was determined to get better. Soon, he was strong enough to be discharged from the ICU, and he lived for almost another two months after his release.

My heart and soul were filled with gratitude. I was so thankful that my sisters and I were able to surround our father with love and care when he needed it the most. The love he received from family and friends was monumental, and it willed him to live as long as he could. Empathy and compassion gave him life and gave us time to be with him in love and light.

Embrace those you love consistently and exhibit kind and loving gestures frequently. We are here for a moment in time; make it memorable. Make it beautiful. Lead with kindness.

The Lord is gracious and righteous; our God is full of compassion.
—Psalm 116:5, NIV

Songs for Empathy and Compassion

Begin your journey to empathy and compassion with kindness, care, and purposeful statements. Here is a powerful song of faith, along with an instrumental selection and two secular hits to help you focus as you journal:

- ○ *Song of faith*
  - – "Keep Me In The Moment" by Jeremy Camp
- ○ *Instrumental music*
  - – "The Wolf & The Moon," most epic music ever by BrunuhVille
- ○ *Secular songs*
  - – "Scars to Your Beautiful" by Alessia Cara
  - – "Kill Em With Kindness" by Selena Gomez

Journaling for Empathy and Compassion

I believe and receive empathy and compassion with unwavering faith and envision my life today as:

_____

_____

_____

_____

_____

_____

Jeannie Burgos

_____

_____

_____

_____

_____

_____

_____

_____

_____

_____

_____

_____

_____

_____

_____

_____

_____

Whatever the circumstance, be open and tenderhearted. We often have no idea what other people's struggles are like. You can do so much good just by telling someone, "I'm here for you. I know you must be going through a lot, and I have you in my thoughts and my prayers." Compassion is an action. It is something that is done. Take the steps to connect with another person. They might not feel like they can talk about their experience, but they still want someone to offer sympathy and understanding. Surprise them with unexpected love and kindness.

> *Hold another up by extending a branch*
> *of compassion and faith.*
> —Jeannie Burgos

Poem for Empathy and Compassion

Compassion and empathy ignite the heart to beat with sympathy;
They offer kindness, humbleness, and sincerity.
Be keen to put forth your personal boundaries,
To not lose yourself in others' stories, needs, and worries.

Compassion is the ability to love without fear,
To relate without judgment, and to empathize without pride.
It unites us together from far and wide.
It's a shoulder, an ear, a whisper, a tear that brings comfort whether far or near.

Teaching empathy and compassion creates ambassadors for peace,
When we see the world through another's eyes, our blessings shall increase,
Our shared compassion joins us in the bonds of community,
For one day we may find that we're the one who needs empathy.

Photo by Aleida Rivera

CHAPTER 12

December: The Spirit of Generosity

There is one who scatters, yet increases more; and there is one who withholds more than is right, but it leads to poverty. The generous soul will be made rich, and he who waters will also be watered himself.
—Proverbs 11:24–25, NKJV

For the Month of December

This month, look for opportunities to be generous. Make a kind gesture and experience the joy of giving. Surrender the expectancy of being recompensed. When you offer your time, your money, and your heart, rest that it may be favored in multitude and come back to you in ways that you cannot foresee. Joyfully receive the love from your goodwill with an open heart.

Think of the pleasure you will feel when you do something kind for a friend, a family member, a colleague, or even a stranger. Imagine the look of love on their face when you tell them not to pay you back but instead to pay it forward to someone else. There are many ways to give that will not cost you money but will still make an impact on someone else's life.

To Achieve the Spirit of Generosity through Unwavering Faith

When you cheerfully give without expectation, it brings inspired happiness into your life and the lives of those around you. This selfless act of giving allows your relationships to grow and blossom. Giving is considered to be a spiritual gift. If God has given you much, you can serve Him by sharing it with others. Surrender your desire to receive in return. Ask yourself the question, *"Who can I bless with my abilities? How can I make a difference in other people's lives?"*

Look for ways to serve. Give the gift of quality time and emotional support. If your friends and family live in abundance, volunteer your time to help those less fortunate. Caring unconditionally for someone else frees you from many of the worries in your own life. No matter how much you have going on, when you take the time to help others with their struggles, it redirects your mind from dwelling on your own problems.

Thought

Some people are concerned about performing acts of generosity because they don't have much to offer. They think, *I'm just living paycheck to paycheck. What do I have that anyone else will want?* Giving doesn't necessarily mean spending money. There is so much more to give than financial resources.

You can give someone else your time, which is the ultimate resource. You can give others a listening ear and a shoulder to cry on when they are going through a difficult period in their lives. You can give them your loving advice when they feel lost. You never know how much good you can bring to someone else's day with a warm smile, a hug, and some caring words.

Truth in Wisdom

What I have experienced to be true is when I start my mornings with thankful prayer, humility, and generous attention for others, it has been a key element to attaining heartened bliss. Giving freely what I can without expecting recognition or praise, especially for those in need, is a personal step closer to knowing God's purpose for me.

I am fully aware that the gesture may not be returned; giving from the heart and surrendering with an open hand is an act of love. Peace and joy will follow, and that is reward enough. When I give without expectation, it's with love: the gift of a smile, the embrace of appreciation, the joy in their eyes is compensation. I may encounter hearts that want to give back, and I accept graciously; however, I also invite them to pay it forward and spread kindness to someone else in need.

Trust in Action

This month, take time to volunteer at an organization that needs your assistance. Helping strangers is one of the purest and most rewarding forms of giving. Volunteer at a church, a soup kitchen, or a local charity. Offer to assist someone who is elderly with everyday tasks that they find difficult. Spend time at an animal shelter to care and find homes for abandoned pets.

By sharing your time and talents, you will offer those in need the reassurance that they are seen, loved, and accepted. If you have financial abundance to give, you can donate to a foundation that needs your support. Give to a charity that supports children in impoverished areas of the country and the world. It is a blessing to be able to save a life. The more you give, the more open your heart will be for others. Joy and abundance is sure to follow.

Visual Belief

As children, we are pure in heart and spirit, and we desire to make others happy. Recall a time from your childhood when you gave someone an unexpected gift. Remember how your heart filled with joy as you watched their eyes widen in delight. Your generosity ignited the spirit of giving and receiving. Their elation was infectious. Savor that feeling. Experience the purity of it. That is the state you will rediscover when you cultivate the spirit of generosity and giving without expectation.

Recognize

Many of us have so much going on in our lives that taking time to charity on a regular basis doesn't appear on our list. As children, we apply these acts of kindness easily and frequently. As we get older, and experience life, we question and we may think to ourselves, *"What's in it for me? Why should I be generous just because it's a nice thing to do?"* Understand that it takes surrendering to give to others without keeping a tally.

Once you discover how good it feels to give, you will be open to receive unexpected blessings. Miracles will show up in rapid form, and you will seek out opportunities to be selfless. The spirit of generosity transforms you into a better family member, friend, and colleague. Making a difference in someone's life, especially at a time when they are in need, brings you closer to the divine. John Bunyan once said, "You have not lived today until you have done something for someone who can never repay you."

True Story of Unwavering Faith

In Acts 20:35, we're reminded of the importance of generosity. *"I have shown you in every way, by laboring like this, that you must support the weak."* And remember the words of the Lord Jesus, that He said, *"It is more blessed to give than to receive"* (NKJV).

I learned the power of generosity when I was about five or six years old. Even at a tender age, I felt a rush of happy energy from giving. As a child, I collected coins by doing little chores, and when family members would offer me a quarter here or a dime there, I made sure to keep this change for special occasions. I saved up for months, and eventually I had enough to make five dollars. Mother's Day was fast approaching, and I vividly remember the excitement of going to the discount store to shop for my mom and grandmother. As I glanced around the shop, I saw two rings. One was a moon and one was a star. I knew right away that would be their surprise. The attendant had a big smile on her face as she presented the rings to me.

I recall saying cheerfully "Yes, I want this for my mommy and abuelita." She took the bag of coins, emptied it on the counter and said I had the exact change for the rings. It was a pivotal moment in my young life. I was blessed. I grew my generous wings that day.

I can still recall how excited I was when I presented my mom and grandmother with their gifts. They were surprised and grateful for this act of kindness. The response I received captivated me and filled me with joy. I am grateful that I discovered the spirit of generosity at such a young age. I am a giving soul for life. It is a lifestyle. If we give freely, we receive freely. When we give from the heart through demonstration of love, compassion and kindness, it's a natural confidence builder and a natural repellant of self-hatred.

I have also learned the hard way by giving in hopes of receiving love in return. For many years of my life, I was not watchful for those showing up to use me for my generosity. With wisdom gained over time and many stumbles, I became more vigilant to let go when I offer a gift. It is a surrender—regardless of whether a person wishes to give in return, provision will come without expectancy.

As you become more and more faithful, embrace God as your provider, and give joyfully. Be generous with an open heart and faithful with a grateful spirit.

Each of you should give what you have decided in your heart to give,
not reluctantly or under compulsion, for God loves a cheerful giver.
—2 Corinthians 9:7, NIV

Songs for the Spirit of Generosity

Begin your journey to the spirit of generosity with kindness, joy, and loving statements. Here is a powerful song of faith, along with an instrumental selection and two secular hits to help you focus as you journal:

- o *Song of faith*
  - – "Undertow" by Danny Gokey
- o *Instrumental music*
  - – "Dreamwalker" by JT Peterson
- o *Secular songs*
  - – "Humble and Kind" by Tim McGraw
  - – "I Hope You Dance" by Lee Ann Womack

Journaling for the Spirit of Giving

I believe and receive the spirit of giving with unwavering faith and envision my life today as:

_____

_____

_____

_____

_____

Jeannie Burgos

Acts of kindness unite us as a community. We get to see the goodness in people's hearts. Giving becomes contagious. The more you give, the more you inspire others to become involved in acts of generosity. You will inspire your children, your neighbors, your classmates, your colleagues to engage in charity. The spirit of generosity is a virtue of giving, not taking; however, what you receive in return is priceless.

Give with an open, generous, and elated
heart for the return is invaluable.
—Jeannie Burgos

Poem for the Spirit of Giving

Give with a spirit of generosity.
Shower from the heart without expectancy.
Recognize the benefits; it's a blessing; an awakening.
An act of kindness that is everlasting.

Breathe in peace and practice creative gifting.
As you serve, teach, explore, and give more.
Surrender the desire for approval and recognition,
And give with sincere and heartfelt intention.

Love is to know and experience.
When you contribute from the heart, it is at its purest.
God rewards those who practice generosity.
Build the bridge of charity and it will hold for eternity.

God is your witness, and there is no other you need to please.
When you give without expectation, you give wings to souls in need.

Photo by Jeannie Burgos

SELF-LOVE EXERCISES

Here are twenty inspiring vows to live by. Incorporate and elaborate your own desired promises. Make yourself a priority. Read them frequently throughout the year. You will see your life transform and your aspirations become a reality.

1. I vow to nurture and practice unwavering faith.
2. I vow to honor my spiritual path and create an amazing life.
3. I vow to know and embrace my worth.
4. I vow to shift physical activity into a daily habit.
5. I vow to treat people how I want to be treated.
6. I vow to live in the moment.
7. I vow to love myself every day.
8. I vow to put my desires into action.
9. I vow to transform my space to suit my vision.
10. I vow to dive into my creativity and discover my talents.
11. I vow to take the time to smell the roses.
12. I vow to travel and explore life.
13. I vow to live in gratitude.
14. I vow to forgive and let go.
15. I vow to challenge myself.
16. I vow to continue to educate myself and level up.
17. I vow to live my best life.
18. I vow to accomplish at least three major intentions each year.
19. I vow to keep a progress journal and chart my triumphs.
20. I vow to pay it forward and encourage; to support, and inspire for good.

HOW I DEVELOPED THIS GUIDED JOURNAL

Days, weeks, months, and years of my life passed as I yearned for something more I worried my days away, and in the midst of heartache, I knew I had to change to see a change. For I was experiencing the opposite of what I wanted, which came fast and furious—many problems, heartaches, troubles, major disappointments, and lack of abundance followed me like a shadow. At times, I felt hopeless, defeated, and discouraged; however, I camouflaged it beautifully. No one knew the inner battle I struggled with. However, I would often lie awake and ask, "Is this it? Is this my life? Why me? When will I get a break? Why aren't my relationships working?"

Then one day, I woke up and said, "*Enough*! Enough of the victimhood, enough of not accepting responsibility, enough of blaming others for not receiving, enough of allowing bad behavior—*enough*."

True change had to emerge before I could receive the answers I so urgently craved. I desired better, and I had to find the way to achieve a new life—a new beginning. I instinctively knew that life had more to offer me, but I didn't have the awareness, the methods, or the solutions to shift from where my mindset resided to where I wanted to be.

I began to do my internal mind work and is now a lifestyle journey. I decisively open myself to truth and love. I take responsibility for my actions and embrace the lessons from the good and unfavorable. As I explore this inner freedom, I discover the beauty of life and what's to come. Dreams that were stagnant and ready to flourish; goals bursting with intention; and joy that is here and now.

141

I challenged old beliefs that did not benefit me and asked revealing questions: *Have I allowed doubt and fear to hold me back from achieving limitless possibilities? What if I can manifest anything I desire the moment that I give my dream direction? What if I stop merely existing and begin to recognize my life as the gift that it is? What if I sincerely give it my all and see what I am made of?*

What I know for sure is that the answer to all of these questions is absolute *faith*. Never give up on yourself! Once you become aware of your true authentic self—what you are passionate about, what you can't walk away from—you will be on your way to achieving your heart's desire. You will finally know what true freedom is—the freedom to design your life.

My desire is to positively inspire. My wish for you is that you see yourself as a *true creator of your life*. Become receptive to God's whisper and guidance. Live courageously and walk through the fire of your own fear. May the blessings show up in all areas of your life day in and day out.

What a gift it will be when you look back in a month, six months, a year from now, fully aware and living the life you have always wanted. May you discover the gift of *Unwavering Faith* and the freedom to design your life, one moment at a time.

ABOUT THE AUTHOR

Photo by Jeannie Burgos

Jeannie Burgos arose from humble beginnings. Born in Brooklyn and raised in Queens, New York, she had little, but her dreams were always ambitious. Inspired by travel, culture, and the realization that we are all God's creations, her faith became the link and miracle to design her life.

Jeannie is the author of *Unwavering Faith*—a thought-provoking, inspirational guide book that shows readers how to manifest positive change through inner belief and faith in God.

Jeannie is a sole proprietor of Dream Events by Jeannie, an organization that raises money for natural disasters and supports foundations that aid children who are victims of abuse, neglect, and homelessness. She has supported C-level executives for over thirty plus years, and for the past eleven years, she has worked as the executive assistant manager to the President and CEO of a Bank. She volunteers for Make a Wish Foundation, MJHS (Hospice Care) / Meals on Wheels, she has volunteered as a Court Appointed Special Advocate (CASA).

Made in the USA
Middletown, DE
31 January 2022